Visions of a Basque American Wes

International Perspectives on the Wr

Frank Bergon

Visions of a Basque American Westerner

INTERNATIONAL PERSPECTIVES ON THE WRITINGS OF

FRANK BERGON

Edited by
Xabier Irujo and Iñaki Arrieta Baro

With an introduction by
Frank Bergon

Center for Basque Studies Press
University of Nevada, Reno
2020

Conference Papers Series, No. 17

Series Editor: Sandra Ott

Center for Basque Studies

University of Nevada, Reno

Reno, Nevada 89557

http://basque.unr.edu

Visions of a Basque American Westerner

International Perspectives on the Writings of Frank Bergon

Cover portrait by Madeline Bergon

Cover design by Rebecca Cross

Library of Congress Cataloging-in-Publication Data

Names: Visions of a Basque American westerner (2019 : University of Nevada, Reno) | Arrieta Baro,
Iñaki,1976-editor. | Irujo Ametzaga, Xabier, editor. | Bergon, Frank, writer of introduction.
Title: Visions of a Basque American westerner : international perspectives on the writings of Frank
Bergon / edited by Xabier Irujo and Iñaki Arrieta ; with an introduction by Frank Bergon.
Description: Reno : Center for Basque Studies Press, University of Nevada, 2020. | Series: Conference
papers series ; no. 17 | Includes bibliographical references. | Summary: "Visions of a Basque American
Westerner: International Perspectives on the Writings of Frank Bergon gathers the essays of nine scholars
and writers from the United States and Europe who presented papers on the novels, essays, and critical
works of Frank Bergon at a two-day conference, sponsored by the Center for Basque Studies and the Jon
Bilbao Basque Library at the University of Nevada, Reno, in March 2019. Topics range from Basque
aspects of Bergon's fiction to his investigation of inauthenticity in a post-truth world, from discussions
of Shoshone Mike as a "perfect novel" to work on The Journals of Lewis and Clark as a "dazzling and
foundational account" in literary ecocriticism. A focus on Bergon's fiction reveals his uniqueness as the
only novelist to present Basque American experience linearly across four generations and the first to render
fully the voices of Okie California since The Grapes of Wrath"-- Provided by publisher.
Identifiers: LCCN 2020024691 | ISBN 9781949805192 (paperback)
Subjects: LCSH: Bergon, Frank--Criticism and interpretation--Congresses.
Classification: LCC PS3552.E71935 Z95 2020 | DDC 813/.54--dc23

LC record available at https://lccn.loc.gov/2020024691

CONTENTS

BOOKS BY FRANK BERGON

Introduction

Frank Bergon

This book began with a surprise phone call from the Basque scholar Joseba Zulaika, who wanted to talk about the antinuke desert monks in one of my novels and the religious anti-drone activists he was writing about. During our conversation, I mentioned that my wife, Holly, and I would soon visit my cousins in Reno. With an outburst of spontaneous Basque generosity, Joseba said, "Oh, you must give a talk at the Center." At that talk, titled "Adventures of a Basque American Novelist," I met Xabier Irujo, Director of the William A. Douglass Center for Basque Studies, and Iñaki Arrieta Baro, the Basque Librarian, who together with Kathlin Ray, Dean of Libraries at the University of Nevada, Reno, welcomed the donation of my papers to the Jon Bilbao Basque Library.

What my talk revealed was that both my mother's Basque ethnicity and my father's Béarnais heritage were subjects of study at the Center for Basque Studies. In fact, the scholar Sandra Ott had written about some of my Béarnais relatives who were Second World War resisters imprisoned in Nazi camps. My intertwined Basque and Béarnais immigrant heritage and writings were seen as contributing to the international cultural history of the American West. I became happily recognized as a specimen.

Another surprise occurred when word came to me that Xabier and Iñaki had begun planning an international conference about my work. The surprise doubled when I learned the planners didn't know that on campus, not far from their offices, the University of Nevada Press was in the process of publishing my latest book. The publication date was then moved to coincide with the two-day conference, at which four Basque and five American scholars and writers gave talks, here revised and published as essays.

A request for me to write the Introduction to this book kept the surprises rolling in. Doubling down on surprise, I decided not to introduce these essays in a traditional way but to let them speak for themselves in all their richness and variety. The two principles I've fabricated for this occasion are to give readers a sense of each writer's primary concerns followed by an illuminating aspect of each essay that surprised me.

Promptly invited from the Basque Country to participate in the conference were the scholars David Rio and Monika Madinabeitia, who over the years in their writings and conferences have been the most active interpreters of literature in relation to Basques in the American West. In their essays, both Madinabeitia and Rio examine Basque elements in my fiction.

In "The Basque World in Frank Bergon's Fiction," Madinabeitia explores Basque identity in its variations over four generations in four of my novels, ranging from the early twentieth century to the present. She rewards readers with a helpful introduction to diaspora scholarship, while chiding so-called new western historians of the past thirty years for their disregard of Basque experience. Her skillful analysis of the novels shows how the word "Basco" in its evolution from a slur to a trendy expression of ethnic pride ranges over multiple ways of being Basque. What surprised me was her claim that so far no other novelist has orchestrated such a linear history of the Basque American experience in the West.

David Rio, as indicated in his aptly titled "Frank Bergon's Western and Basque American Heroes: Deconstructing Archetypes," performs a double task in analyzing how the novels challenge both Basque American and American western male stereotypes. His erudition allows him to identify the revisionist aspect of masculinity in the novels: their antiheroes depart from overlapping conventional views of western toughness and Basque *indarra*, a word meaning endurance and fortitude as well as physical strength. Rio's precise and insightful character analysis yielded a shock of recognition for me in his revelation that all my novels have double male protagonists, the two often forming a bond, even in conflict.

Like both preceding Basque scholars, the American writer William Heath ranges over all four novels in "The Real Thing: Authenticity in Frank Bergon's Fiction," with a differing emphasis on the craft of fiction. Sensuous details, appropriate points of view, and credible narrative voices give fiction its authority, along with style, which isn't like frosting on a cake but fiction's determinant ingredient, as Heath points out when observing what book reviewers miss: style reveals the natural world as a chief character in these novels. His perspicacious detailing of characters and events gives importance to women, suggesting a future study might focus on the power these women exhibit in the fictional worlds they inhabit. New for me was seeing how each novel features an anachronistic and controversial way of life, leaving me to ponder the significance of nomadic Indians, desert monks, mountain men, and fighting farm boys in terms of my future subject matter.

Sylvan Goldberg turns from fiction to nonfiction in "Fictive Truths: Frank Bergon's Literary Critique in a Post-Truth World." From his perspective in the twenty-first century, Goldberg digs back through five decades of my critical writing to discover how the question of authenticity is central to all of it. His assured comprehension of American western and ecocritical studies grounds his perception of what's innovative in discussions of authenticity in a post-authentic world, whether about Lewis and Clark's journals in the West or John Burroughs's natural history essays in the East. His valiant research shows how an awareness of the inseparable link between imagination and material fact, each giving shape to the other, can generate literary activism in a world of unstable truths. A shock to me was how constant he showed this guiding principle to exist through years of writing about subjects as different as Stephen Crane's fiction and the Zapatista Indians of Chiapas.

The shards and detritus of a career producing the fiction and nonfiction so far discussed are the subject of Iñaki Arrieta Baro's, "Frank Bergon's Papers: A Multifaceted Archival Collection." To start with a surprise: unaware of rules and proposals for naming archival papers, I followed Dean Kathy Ray's suggestion for a specific name and am happy to learn it meets the official criteria of *DACS* 2.3.19. Arrieta Baro, a most thoughtful and patient librarian, tolerated my inability to predict the size or contents of the collection and guided me through the process of submission, generously telling me that anything related to biography was acceptable. When most authors' papers remain for years in unsorted archival boxes, the real surprise came with Arrieta Baro's quick organization and documentation of so much of this collection, resulting in a splendid library exhibit at the time of the conference.

In their essays, Joseba Zulaika, Zeese Papanikolas, and David Means focus on individual novels. *The Temptations of St. Ed & Brother S* couldn't have a better reader than Zulaika, a former monk and current activist, whose scholarship always combines the public and personal, the intertwining of ethnography and memoir, as in his lively books about Basque violence and the city of Bilbao. In his essay, "Apocalypse and Transfiguration in Nevada's Nuclear Test Site: Frank Bergon's Desert of the Real," Zulaika draws parallels between my fictionalized Cistercian and Carmelite monks and the Franciscan, Jesuit, and Catholic Worker activists he encountered. I was gratified to discover that the religious and political dilemmas facing my antinuke monks twenty-five years ago still illumine today's hyperreality of 9/11, drone warfare, Trump's fantastical presidency, and Las Vegas as a mirage of the sublime. Most gratifying and surprising was how my rendition of monastic spirituality caused Zulaika to wonder if I'd ever been a monk.

Zeese Papanikolas also devotes a sensitive reading to a single novel in "Unheard Voices of Okie California." As someone who knows the field, he points out a great novelistic silence about California's migrant Okies after the 1939 publication of Steinbeck's *The Grapes of Wrath*. These Okie voices, heard in the songs of Merle Haggard, Buck Owens, and Doye O'Dell, reemerge in the youthful characters of *Jesse's Ghost*, the assimilated, second-generation sons and daughters of Steinbeck's Okies, who internalize their parents' social stigma of being told: you're not good enough, you're still second pickings. Their responses in a tough fistfighting world, as Papanikolas shows, create a world of violence intertwined with love, tenderness, and grace. Papanikolas surprisingly places the story in a long literary tradition of brotherly friendship when he shows how an event in the novel mirrors one in the *Iliad*, a scene not conscious to me while writing, but one I'd read in high school Greek class.

In "Frank Bergon: Dreaming the American West," David Means explores how the imagination works in two novels based on documented physical violence in a western landscape. In a startling amalgam of what used to be called biographical and historical literary criticism, Means presents an original shift in emphasis from authorial and historical facts to the imaginative leap beyond facts that produces retrospective fictive visions. His own thirty years as a fiction writer enter his description of the intuitive dream mode he has experienced and perceives even in fact-based and autobiographical novels. His essay duplicates the imaginative process he describes as he ruminates about *Shoshone Mike* and reminisces about *Jesse's Ghost*, unexpectedly connecting us beyond our role as friends to writers sharing a method. The similarity he identifies between the characters and vision in my two novels and those in the plays of a third writer, Sam Shepard, was surprising until he quoted a nighttime soliloquy in my novel that connected us through what Means demonstrates is the poetic power of fictional language.

Nancy Cook conducts a thorough investigation of my writings about California, both published and unpublished, in "Long Shadows Across the

Valley: Regarding Difference, Work, and Community in Frank Bergon's California." Shadowy negotiations over status and power, occluded for the characters in *Jesse's Ghost*, become knowable for readers when glimpsed through Cook's revealing lens of social class struggles. Her lucent reading of a scene involving an Okie kid's observation of an encounter between a Basque American woman and an African American ranch hand provides a lesson in understanding subtextual social politics conveyed by an unreliable narrator. Cook's own ranching experience informs her view of community and communal values in my most recent book, *Two-Buck Chuck & The Marlboro Man: The New Old West*, where the valley's hard-won porous social boundaries are best exhibited in the democratic affiliations of the boarders' table at the Basque Hotel.

Cook's essay ends this book with a surprising revelation about a desire spanning much of my life as a writer. Her discussion of *Two-Buck Chuck & The Marlboro Man* shows how the book presents a range of portraits that profiles the San Joaquin Valley as a region of extreme racial and ethnic diversity. While recently submitting my archives to the Basque Library, I discovered to my surprise the stirrings of this book in a proposal I wrote for an undergraduate senior-year project as a newly appointed Scholar of the College. In the proposal, I offered a plan to write a collection of stories about the agricultural San Joaquin Valley that included a mix of African Americans, Russian Molokans, and Dust Bowl Okie migrants, "Mexicans unrecognized as Americans in California and unrecognized as Mexicans in Mexico," as well as those of Basque, Japanese, Armenian, and Filipino heritage. As one of my characters might say, after fifty-five years, that's what I've finally gone and done.

The ranch country where I grew up was often rough and violent, but it was ruled by a moral code of reciprocity. If someone gave you something, you gave back. If someone did you a favor, you returned it. This primal code of behavior broke down when a gift was of such generosity—as these essays are for me—that reciprocation fails. There was one response I learned I could offer then, as now: my gratitude.

The Basque World in Frank Bergon's Fiction

Monika Madinabeitia

> People from the West—Nevada or Idaho or California's
> San Joaquin Valley—knew right off from his last name
> . . . that he was Basque.
>
> —Frank Bergon, *Wild Game*

Erramouspe, Arrizabalaga, Irigaray, and Etcheverry are the surnames of the main Basque characters in Frank Bergon's four novels: Jean Erramouspe in *Shoshone Mike* (1987),[1] St. Ed Arrizabalaga in *The Temptations of St. Ed & Brother S* (1993),[2] Jack Irigaray in *Wild Game* (1995),[3] and Mitch Etcheverry in *Jesse's Ghost* (2011).[4] These characters represent the arrival and settlement of Basques from frontier days to the contemporary American West. They embody many Basque American stories and images but are also clear manifestations of the different ways of being and understanding what it is to be Basque in the American West. Certainly, these different representations of Basqueness also underscore the need to revisit Basque identity in the homeland.

Frank Bergon is both committed and entitled to write about Basques in the American West because of his own firsthand experience. Bergon's maternal grandparents left their hometowns in Euskal Herria around the turn of the twentieth century and eventually settled in Nevada. As Bergon explains, "My Basque grandparents settled in the state of Nevada, where my grandfather had worked briefly with sheep and later in the mines. In the small town of Battle Mountain, my grandparents owned a hotel and a grocery store that catered to Basques."[5] Bergon was born in 1943 in Ely, Nevada, but when he was only a child his family moved to the San

---

1   Frank Bergon, *Shoshone Mike* (New York: Penguin Books, [1987] 1991).
2   Frank Bergon, *The Temptations of St. Ed & Brother S.* (Nevada: University of Nevada Press, 1993).
3   Frank Bergon, *Wild Game* (Nevada: University of Nevada Press, 1995).
4   Frank Bergon, *Jesse's Ghost* (Berkeley: Heyday, 2011).
5   Monika Madinabeitia, "Getting to Know Frank Bergon," *Society of Basque Studies in America*, 28 (2008), 71.

Joaquin Valley in California. Although Bergon has lived in the East and Colorado for many years, Nevada and California have undoubtedly shaped his Basque and western identity, as can be extracted from his fiction and narrative in general.

Bergon's fiction conveys a unique revision of the transition from immigrant to diasporic experience, from invisibility to visibility. Although "there is still no satisfactory answer to the closely related question of why and when migrants form new diasporic entities or join existing ones,"[6] these four novels expose the "ethno-genesis"[7] of the Basque community and their initiation journey into their ultimate growth as an ingrained element of the American West, as an established and acknowledged diaspora.[8] Bergon has cunningly outlined this mutation through the term "Basco," as will be revealed in this essay.

Shoshone Mike deals with first- and second-generation Basques, a stage that "the perceiver does not belong to."[9] The novel explores how, "[d]uring an ethnic group's early period in the United States, its members are too diffident about their place in the new society to assert their identity with vigor."[10] By re-creating the true event of the so-called "Last Indian Battle," *Shoshone Mike* recalls the distress that the Basque community largely underwent as foreigners on American land. In the tragedy, which occurred in northern Nevada in 1911, three Basque shepherds and an Anglo were killed by a Shoshone family. Afterward the Shoshone family was pursued and almost all were killed by a posse of white men. Bergon presents his fictionalized version of this story and revises the paradigms of "regeneration through violence"[11] found in the common Anglo-versus-Native American dichotomy. The novelty is that Bergon also contemplates an Anglo-versus-Basque connection, the friction of time, as a product of his extensive research and firsthand experience as a Basque American. There are so far three

---

6   Gabriel Sheffer, *Diaspora Politics* (Cambridge: Cambridge University Press, [2003] 2006), 16.
7   Ibid., 17.
8   See Gloria Totoricagüena's *Basque Diaspora*, especially "Defining 'Diaspora' " and "Other Ethnic Diasporas" (Reno: Center for Basque Studies, 2004); Agustin M. Oiarzabal and Pedro J. Oiarzabal's *La Identidad Vasca en El Mundo* (Bilbao: Erroteta, 2005) or Argitxu Camus Etchecopar's "Diaspora and Ethnicity" in *The North American Basque Organizations (NABO), Incorporated/ Ipar Amerikako Euskal Elkarteak, 1973-2007* (Gasteiz: Urazandi Bilduma, Eusko Jaurlaritzaren Argitalpen Zerbitzu Nagusia, 2007), 45-53.
9   Marilyn B. Brewer, *Intergroup Relations* (Buckingham: Open University Press, [1996] 2003), 131.
10   Richard D. Alba, *Ethnic Identity* (New Haven: Yale University Press, 1990) 29.
11   Richard Slotkin, *Regeneration Through Violence: The Mythology of the American Frontier, 1600-1860* (Hanover: Wesleyan University Press, 1973).

other books/novels written about the events. The first full-length study was Kenneth Scott's *Frozen Grass* (1960); then came Effie Mona Mack's *The Indian Massacre of 1911 at Little High Rock Canyon* (1968); and eventually, Dayton O. Hyde's book, *The Last Free Man: The True Story Behind the Massacre of Shoshone Mike and His Band of Indians in 1911* (1973). The novelty is that Bergon also contemplates an Anglo-versus-Basque connection, the friction of the time, as a product of his extensive research, and Hyde even suggests that the Shoshone women were molested by the Basque men to explain why the Shoshone killed them. Bergon was outraged, since Hyde's accusations were presented as facts, with no evidence. While researching *Shoshone Mike*, Bergon tried to get in touch with Hyde. He never got a reply. I tried to do the same in 2010 and received no answer either. One possible explanation for Hyde's speculations could be his own experience as a cowboy and rancher. Hyde probably favored the cattlemen and thus felt aversion toward the herders—Basques. Hyde seems to reproduce an earlier stereotypical view of Basques, who had only recently become visible in the American mainstream. Basques had not populated the pages of frontier history, nor the big screen,[12] and were even forgotten by the new western historians in landmark books like Patricia Limerick's *The Legacy of Conquest* (1987),[13] as well as others.[14]

Shoshone Mike captures the ethnic customs of first-generation Basques, who usually gathered in close circles and whose interaction with Anglos was scarce. Most of them spoke very little English, which reinforced their alien status and limited their job opportunities. Since herding sheep did not require linguistic skills and was a job that no one wanted, many Basque men were able to herd sheep in the desert. This is the case of Jean Erramouspe's father, Pete, one of the dead shepherds, who "ended up on the range with a band of sheep and no dogs. Pete said nothing because he could speak no English."[15] Bergon's explicit re-creation of first-generation Basques includes the use of a few Basque words and sentences in some of their conversations, as in "Zer gertatzen da?"[16] or "txakurrak."[17] The novel also reverses the stereotype of Basque shepherds overseas as skilled. Pete

---

12   See Óscar Álvarez Gila and Iker Arranz Otaegui's "La Imagen del Inmigrante Vasco en El Cine," *Revista de Letras y Ficción Audiovisual* 4 (2014), 68-96.

13   Patricia N. Limerick, *The Legacy of Conquest* (New York: W. W. Norton and Company, Inc., 1987).

14   Frederick C. Luebke, "Introduction," in *European Immigrants in The American West* (Albuquerque: University of New Mexico Press, 1998), vii-viii.

15   *Shoshone Mike*, 22.

16   Ibid., 45.

17   Ibid., 22.

unveils how he knew nothing about herding sheep upon his arrival in the American West but how his first boss assumed he was fully qualified just because he was Basque. He claims, "I didn't know what I was supposed to do . . . I ran through sagebrush pleading with two thousand sheep to stay together . . . but they scattered";[18] in fact, "Everything [Pete] knew about sheep he'd learned after coming to America."[19]

Besides shepherding, boarding houses are now conceived as another salient ethnic marker of Basques in the American West. They initially operated as boarding houses, often called Basque Hotels, and were usually the closest thing to the Basque home for early-generation Basques; to many they were a "[h]ome away from home."[20] They lodged countless Basques upon arrival; they also accommodated countless lonely shepherds and often took in sick shepherds. Although many fared well, there are numberless tragic stories of people losing their minds, usually because of the harshness of the desert and its solitude;[21] "Crazy Bascos" were often called "Sheeped" or "Sagebrushed."[22] Far from the romantic view often attached to the Basque community, *Shoshone Mike* unmasks the reality of many of the people who had come to America, gone insane, and lost everything, even their lives. This is the case of the old shepherd who lives in the Basque Hotel in Winnemucca. He went crazy after a "freak blizzard";[23] people say " 'he was a fine shepherd. . . . He left everything behind. Now he has nothing.' "[24] This Basque Hotel reveals other common features within the Basque community, like card games, months-old Basque newspapers, shepherds laid off for the winter with no prospect until shearing or lambing in the spring, or their Catholic nature and practices.[25]

Pete left his hometown in the late nineteenth century. He married another Basque, as was customary at that stage of Basque establishment in the West. Intermarriages between different ethnic groups and communities would come later. Jean Erramouspe was thus born in a Basque home of the American West. In the novel, we learn that, unlike his father, he works in the mines. Bergon includes this disruptive element as evidence of the

18   Ibid.
19   Ibid., 24.
20   Jeronima Echeverria, *Home Away from Home* (Reno: University of Nevada Press, 1999).
21   See "VIII. Artzainen Neke eta Arriskuak," in Asun Garikano´s *Far Westeko Euskal Herria* (Iruñea: Pamiela, 2009).
22   Richard H. Lane and William A. Douglass, *Basque Sheepherders of the American West* (Reno: University of Nevada Press, 1985), 29.
23   *Shoshone Mike*, 44.
24   Ibid., 45.
25   Ibid., 44

professional heterogeneity within the Basque collectivity, particularly among the second generation, despite the commonplace equation of Basques with shepherds.[26] Chain migration is one reason that the sheep-ranching industry became an important economic focus for Basque immigrants.[27] In fact, the Basque community in Surprise Valley—where the events took place—was largely from Banca, in the French Basque Country, and some of them were even family members. This family connection is re-created in the novel, since all the deceased Basques were from Banca. Similarly, Erramouspe has two uncles in the area: John Laxague, another of the deceased herders, and Paul Itzaina.

Many second-generation Basques were picked on because of their Basque roots. The novel illustrates some of the derogatory terms, such as the expression "Basco." Defamatory phrases such as "Everyone knows they put Bascos out with sheep 'cuz the smell keeps the coyotes away"[28] exemplify the adversities that many Basques underwent until they were eventually accepted into the mainstream. Father Enright, the priest of Winnemucca, tells Erramouspe to be careful, for "[t]here are no laws now, and the sheriff patrols the range to tax the tramp herds. People are getting impatient with their foreign sheep bands, and it makes it hard for all Basques who come here."[29] Erramouspe desperately replies, "I'm as American as anyone else."[30] Erramouspe is a clear example of how countless American-born Basques rejected their roots and attempted to embrace solely American identity. They were Basques, but not by choice; they wanted to be American. However, back then, Basques were often unacknowledged as such. Basques eagerly sought to assimilate and felt ashamed of where they came from. Erramouspe's character construes the relationship between recognition and identity as well as how "our identity is partly shaped by recognition or its absence, often by the misrecognition of others, and so a person or group of people can suffer real damage, real distortion, if the people or society around them mirror back to them a confining or demeaning or contemptible picture of themselves." In fact, "[n]onrecognition or misrecognition can inflict harm, can be a form of

26 See Iker Saitua's "The Best Sheepherder," *Historia Contemporánea* 56 (2018), 81-119.
27 See Gloria Totoricagüena, *Identity, Culture, and Politics in the Basque Diaspora* (Reno: University of Nevada Press, 2004), 16-17; or Kristina Crawford, "The Chains of Family: Basque Migration and the Archaeological Record," *California Archaeology* 4 (Spring 2012), 55–68.
28 *Shoshone Mike*, 108.
29 Ibid., 46.
30 Ibid.

oppression, imprisoning someone in a false, distorted, and reduced mode of being."[31]

Erramouspe is trapped in a space of "nowhere," for he is involuntarily part of the Basque community, and his affiliation to the American community is unrecognized. This is one of the main differences with Jack Irigaray in *Wild Game*. Irigaray represents the wish of many third-generation Basques to connect with their Basque heritage. Irigaray is fully aware of his two cultures; however, unlike Erramouspe, he is recognized as fully American by his peers and the mainstream. Irigaray's father is a second-generation Basque who, unlike his brother, Uncle Pete, and his own parents, chooses to work in casinos rather than live off the land. Irigaray, the son, is a third-generation Basque, with a university degree, who does not speak Basque, is married to a non-Basque, and has two young daughters. *Wild Game* expresses how Basques became very American and how many became managers, bankers, lawyers, and entrepreneurs.[32] As we learn in this novel, "Laxalt, Arrizabalaga, Ybarguengoitia were familiar names around Reno, but no longer of sheepherders. The solitary Basque herders of previous generations—those tough 'Black Bascos' as they were derisively called— had pretty much vanished."[33]

Wild Game re-creates a true event that took place in the 1980s in Idaho. Bergon's fictionalized version places the novel in both Idaho and Nevada and adds a Basque American as the main character. It describes "New Basques"[34] and explores their changing roles as opposed to those of earlier generations. Immigration to the American West mainly started around 1850.[35] Many Basques felt attracted to the promising news of the Gold Rush in California. However, after encountering disappointment and misfortune, countless Basques turned to herding sheep. They moved to

---

31 Ibid.
32 John Bieter and Mark Bieter, *An Enduring Legacy* (Reno: University of Nevada Press, 2000), 24-25.
33 *Wild Game*, 2-3.
34 William A. Douglass, "A World Eclipsed," *The World and I* (December 1993), 262.
35 See James P. Kelly, *The Settlement of Basques in the American West*, Senior paper, Harvard University, 1967.

other states, like Nevada,[36] Oregon,[37] or Idaho.[38] Basques usually found jobs as shepherds for the reasons enunciated by Pete above. Basques herded sheep until the end of the nineteenth and part of the twentieth century, when federal grazing laws[39] and conflict with cattlemen directly affected their practice.[40] Many left for the Old Country,[41] while others remained in the American West. Among those who stayed, many acquired properties, became ranchers, and hired men to work for them. Some even turned to ranching and stopped sheepherding.[42] During the 1950s, most Basques turned from rural to urban jobs. Irigaray explains that "[m]ost of the Basques [he] grew up with peaceably sold cars, taught school, ran banks, wrote books, even hobnobbed with the president."[43]

---

36 See Iker Saitua, *Basque Immigrants and Nevada's Sheep Industry* (Reno: University of Nevada Press, 2019); Richard H. Lane, "Trouble in the Sweet Promised Land," in *Anglo-American Contributions to Basque Studies*, ed. William A. Douglass, Richard W. Etulain, and William H. Jacobsen, Jr. (Reno: Desert Research Institute on the Social Sciences, 1977).

37 For Oregon, see Richard Wayne Etulain, "Basques," https://oregonencyclopedia. org/articles/basques/#.XCpkulxKjIU; see Etulain, "Basque Beginnings in the Pacific Northwest," *Idaho Yesterdays* 18 (Spring 1979) and *Basques of the Pacific Northwest* (Boise: University of Idaho Press, 1991) for the Pacific Northwest.

38 See Gloria Totoricagüena, "Ethnic Industries for Migrants," *Euskonews & Media* 212, (2003), http://www.euskonews.eus/0212zbk/kosmo21201.html.

39 "In 1934, the United States Congress passed the Taylor Grazing Act, which placed an additional 173 million acres of land into federally controlled grazing districts. The new requirements for grazing on these public lands included paying fees and following a specified schedule for all of those using the land, but most importantly it originated the requirement that all of those wishing to use the federal lands had to establish a base property which they privately owned, in order to be eligible for the public lands grazing rights. Land allocation was determined by government officials and cattle ranchers serving on advisory boards, which were keen to deny access to the itinerant Basque sheepman." Gloria Totoricagüena, "Ethnic Industries for Migrants," *Euskonews & Media* 212, (2003), http://www.euskonews.eus/0212zbk/kosmo21201. html.

40 "Like Native American and Hispanic herders, Basques in the West were widely considered non-white—and at a historical moment when racial identity was fraught, faced suspicion by their very existence. Unlike cowboys who symbolized freedom, sheep herders around the turn of the 20th century represented something undesirable." (Adam M. Sowards, "Why Sheep Started So Many Wars in the American West," *What It Means to Be American*, October 5, 2017, http://www.whatitmeanstobeamerican.org/ identities/why-sheep-started-so-many-wars-in-the-american-west/). The conflict between sheep and cattle is the theory suggested by just a few (like the Nevada historian Phillip Earl) to explain the Last Indian Massacre. According to this theory— not proved to date—Basques were killed by cattlemen because of the grazing dissidence between them, and the Shoshone were then blamed for it. The evidence found by Bergon throughout his extensive research discards this option as plausible.

41 See "IV. Euskal Herrian Berriro" (329-346) in Garikano, *Far Westeko*.

42 Some of the most salient examples are the Altube Brothers and the Garats. See Mike Laughlin, "Basque Ranching Culture in the Great Basin," *Northeastern Historical Society Quarterly*, 3-4 (2010).

43 *Wild Game*, 3.

Irigaray and his two daughters represent the conception of New Basques, which encompasses both American and Basque identity. Irigaray clarifies that when he was a kid "they were all just Americans, and not even hyphenated ones . . . he was just another westerner—a Nevadan."[44] Irigaray's new ethnic awareness translates into action, such as taking his young girls to Basque festivals or to the Zazpiak Bat Reno Basque Club to instill in them a robust and vibrant sense of ethnic identity. Irigaray re-creates the social and cultural context of the time: generally, third-generation Basques felt no individual cost, which allowed Basques not only to be aware of their ethnic identity, but also to claim it and nurture it actively. Erramouspe and Irigaray are inarguable, salient examples of private and public identities and manifestations. While Erramouspe is Basque at home and American in public, Irigaray and his daughters are American at home and Basque in public. Earlier-generation Basques felt the pressure to hide their ethnicity or were not even aware of it. Conversely, third-generation public displays comprise messages and slogans such as "Proud to be Basque," "100% Basque," or even "1/2 Basque is better than none," on T-shirts, license plates or caps.

Consequently, Irigaray illustrates how Basques nowadays proudly express their wish to cling to their roots by participating in rituals and social events, such as dancing or festivals in general. Festivals and rituals explicitly celebrate the identity of the people and become its cultural expression.[45] Festivals permit "the Basque community to project its self-image to non-Basque society. The Basques simultaneously reassert ethnic pride . . . as they acknowledge their membership in the broader American society."[46] Initially the primary aim of festivals was to create a new Basque identity by changing the Basque image from that of a shepherd to that of an American citizen, from an immigrant into a diasporan.[47] In fact, the first Basque festival[48] is regarded as representing the rite of passage of immigrants to an ethnic group, from the mountains to urbanity.[49] Robert Laxalt, one of the organizers of this first festival, contributed to this reformed image by means of his successful *Sweet Promised Land* (1957).[50] Laxalt tells the story of his father, Dominique, who immigrated to America

---

44 Ibid.
45 Kepa Fernández de Larrinoa, "The Western Basque Festival," in *Los Otros Vascos,* ed. Xavier F. Medina (Madrid: Editorial Fundamentos, 1997), 104.
46 William A. Douglass and Jon Bilbao, *Amerikanuak* (Reno: University of Nevada Press, 1975), 391.
47 Fernández, "The Western," 124.
48 The First Basque Festival took place in Sparks, Nevada, in 1959.
49 Fernández, "The Western", 114-115.
50 Robert Laxalt, *Sweet Promised Land* (Reno: University of Nevada Press [1957]2007).

as a youngster. His book narrates the hardships his father encounters as a shepherd, the obstacles to prosper, his solitude in the mountains and desert, as well as his nostalgia for his homeland, his friends, and relatives. After almost 50 years in America, the Laxalt children finally convince their father to go to the Basque Country, accompanied by his son Robert. This memoir ends with the son and the father about to leave the Basque Country and head back for America. Dominique cries, in a mixture of distress and sorrow, that he cannot go back to the Basque Country, that he does not belong there anymore; broken-hearted, he shouts "I can't go back. It ain't my country any more. I've lived too much in America ever to go back."[51] This confession embodies the double identity of many Basque immigrants who became aware that they were foreigners in both countries. Basques were not only un/misrecognized by their host/home countries, but also by themselves. In other words, what they felt or were, or wanted to become, frequently clashed and hence caused an identity crisis and the feeling that they belonged nowhere. They were called "Bascos" in the American West and "Indianuak" or "Amerikanuak" in the Basque Country. Even they themselves failed to recognize who they were because of their cultural division. They often did not know where home was or found out, painfully, that the alien country they lived in had now become their home, as in Dominique's case.

Irigaray represents Basques who have benefited from previous ethnic struggles and have been successful in eventually reconciling both cultures, both homes. While Erramouspe embodies the struggle when it was not safe to be ethnic, Irigaray illustrates how it then became secure, and even trendy, to be ethnic. By then the First Western Basque Festival, Laxalt's *Sweet Promised Land*, and the civil rights movements that fostered ethnic awareness and pride had soaked into the American mainstream. In fact, "[d]uring the 1960s and afterward, it became less fashionable to be simply American—living in what many considered to be a bland, vanilla culture— and increasingly popular to be *from* somewhere, to have an identity that set one apart."[52] *Wild Game* therefore exposes "[t]he principle of third-generation interest," which claims that "What the son wishes to forget, the grandson wishes to remember;"[53] in other words, what Erramouspe wishes to forget, Irigaray wants to remember.

---

51   Ibid., 157-158.
52   Bieter and Bieter, *An Enduring Legacy*, 5.
53   Marcus L. Hansen, *The Problem of the Third Generation Immigrant.* (Rock Island: Augustana Historical Society, 1938), 9.

However, contrary to Erramouspe's life experience, which entails Basque practices on a regular basis—such as being able to speak Basque and actually speaking it with his relatives or other community members— Irigaray's relationship to Basqueness is not a daily fact. His bond, as in the case of many other third- and further-generation Basques, encompasses symbols or emblems that have been associated with Basqueness. This type of connection raises the debate of whether the preservation of the heritage through symbols, emblems, festivals, and dances qualifies one to be Basque. Likewise, it also poses the question of what being Basque means. For example, Irigaray, like many assimilated Basques, does not speak Euskara. Although in the contemporary West, Basque Americans are making a significant effort, many are not linguistically skilled. Third-generation Basques, like Irigaray himself, were born into families where often only one parent was Basque. Equally, many were born into families who rejected their Basque heritage and wanted to dissociate themselves from being Basque. Because of the general un/misrecognition they had gone through, second-generation Basques worked hard to assimilate themselves and wanted the same for their children. That meant that Euskara was consciously not spoken at home and that English prevailed. Besides, Euskara has a reputation for being difficult; thus, to many the effort-reward ratio does not compensate.

Mitch Etcheverry explains that he cannot speak any Basque. His "folks know some, but it's too late for [him] to learn. They say the Devil tried to learn Basque by listening outside a farmhouse, but after seven years he could only say two words: 'Yes, ma'am.' "[54] In other cases, children learned Euskara from their parents and elders in the community, but since it was mainly reduced to home use and the Basque community was shrinking, for since the 1970s the Basque immigration influx into the West had decreased, they had no one to converse with in Euskara.

Uncle Pete, Irigaray's uncle, explains how Basque was his mother tongue when he was a child, but that he has forgotten it.[55] The death of parents or of a fluent Basque-speaking community negatively affected the maintenance of the language. Euskara is certainly an area of discussion: while many in Euskal Herria cling to Euskara as defining Basques, whether this rule should apply to diasporans needs to be debated, particularly when

---

54   *Jesse's Ghost*, 73.
55   *Wild Game*, 85.

the street use of Basque has decreased in the homeland[56]—even though, ironically, more people can actually speak it.

Another distinction between earlier and later-generation Basques is that initially Basques, like the Erramouspe parents, usually married other Basques. Conversely, both St. Ed Arrizabalaga, the abbot in *The Temptations of St. Ed & Brother S*, and Irigaray are married and then divorced from non-Basques, a common current trend at the time of this writing. That is why parents, like Irigaray, try to bind their children to their Basque identity through festivals, dance clubs, choirs, or alike. This indicates the reversal of the original aim of festivals, dance clubs, and Basque centers: they were initially created and promoted to vindicate the Americanness of the Basques.[57] Nowadays, the aim is to counterbalance a strong American identity with a Basque one; in other words, to help more Americanized Basques cling to their original roots, even if only symbolically. In fact, this " 'symbolic ethnicity' offers individuals the opportunity to pick and choose the most appealing aspects of immigrant culture . . . without suffering from ostracism of the stranger and the constant obstacles of language."[58]

Another possibility within the spectrum of Basqueness is not to embrace it at all, or even to ignore it. This would be the case re-created by Arrizabalaga, whose story also takes place in 1980s Nevada. Arrizabalaga does not show any explicit attachment to his Basque heritage, mirroring many Basques who do not publicly show their loyalty towards their ethnicity. This could result from Arrizabalaga's voluntary choice not to associate himself in the collective transformation of becoming/being both Basque and American. Another option could be that he does not see the need to manifest his Basqueness publicly, which does not imply that he does not feel Basque or that he is not aware of his ethnicity. This brings us back to the debate about what it is to be Basque and whether one's own ethnic identity is to be quantified according to the proportion of outward manifestations. This voluntary absence of public affiliation and Arrizabalaga's devoted fight against nuclear energy convey both the connection and diversity of Basques who simultaneously share the same space and time. To put it another way, it portrays different ways of being Basque. In fact, ethnicity can vary from an optional identity to a total identity;[59] that is, Basque

---

56 "VII Measurement of the Street Use of Languages: Basque Country, 2016," Soziolinguistika Klusterra, July 2017 (accessed August 5, 2019).
57 Fernández, "The Western," 124.
58 Nina M. Ray and John P. Bieter, " 'It Broadens Your View of Being Basque': Identity Through History, Branding and Cultural Policy," *International Journal of Cultural Policy, 21*, no. 3 (2015), 2.
59 Totoricagüena, *Identity, Culture, and Politics,* 199.

ethnicity is a matter of choice. This choice involves varying degrees of manifestation, implication, and combination. Similarly, this choice, as in Arrizabalaga's case, includes the nonexistence of public practices, which should not be automatically equated to total denial or ignorance of one's own ethnic identity; it could simply be a personal choice.

Emotional connections to Basque traits or their absence need also to be taken into account, since they can express the level of ethnic affiliation of Basque Americans. For example, although Erramouspe speaks Basque, he tries to publicly hide his skill; on the contrary, although speaking Euskara as a prerequisite for being Basque has lost support in diaspora populations,[60] Irigaray laments his not being able to do so. Erramouspe firmly claims his Americanness and works hard to assimilate into the mainstream. In contrast, Irigaray shows clear signs of total westernization and hence seeks indicators to strengthen his Basqueness. Irigaray does not seek to devitalize his American identity, but he embodies the depersonalized postmodern individual within a technocratic world, an individual who tries to distinguish himself in the mainstream.

This urge to differ from the dominant group is part of the previously mentioned fashion that seeks to avoid the simplicity of being just American. Erramouspe, on the contrary, as someone of the generation preceding the emergence of ethnic pride in the late 1950s, pursues the possibility of simply being American. Erramouspe grew up in the era when they were not to celebrate diversity; rather, they were to eliminate it. Irigaray and his children, although genetically more distant from their Basque roots, represent the New Basques who have clung to culture as a means to perpetuate or (re)generate a Basque identity. In other words, the genetic bond replaces the cultural tie. This "ethnogenetics" phenomenon, as we may call it, as exhibited in Erramouspe's case, is not a rational or free choice; in contrast, Irigaray's and his children's 'ethnoculturalism' is voluntary, it is the outcome of a choice.

Wild Game and *Jesse's Ghost* renovate the romantic image of the Basque shepherd. While *Shoshone Mike* presents the actual era in which herding sheep was common among Basques, Bergon's last novels present the archetypal Basque as part of a bygone era. The deaths of Uncle Pete and Sam Etcheverry illustrate this end. Uncle Pete is "an outmoded figure

---

60   See Gloria Totoricagüena, "The Basque Language Abroad," in *The Legal Status of the Basque Language Today*, ed. Gloria Totoricagüena Egurrola and Iñigo Urrutia Libarona (Donostia: Eusko Ikaskuntza, 2008), 43-72.

tottering on the rim of extinction."[61] His death symbolizes the end of "the tough, lonesome world of Basques herding sheep in desolate hills and buckaroos following chuck wagons and sleeping in bedrolls"[62]—a symbol also applicable to Sam Etcheverry, Mitch's father. These two novels overtly underscore the changing roles of Basques in the American West. Mitch Etcheverry does not follow the occupation of his elders; he leaves the rural West, lives in San Francisco and is now a big-shot newspaperman.[63] Etcheverry's way of being Basque is especially featured in meals at Basque Hotels, which is a form of nostalgic communication with his ancestry without significant impact on his daily life.[64] Food, like other rituals, represents visceral bonds with one's heritage. The visceral, if understood as "sensations, moods and ways of being that emerge from our sensory engagement with the material and discursive environments in which we live,"[65] allows us to pay "attention to the senses—sight, sound, touch, smell and taste—which are a mechanism for visceral arousal."[66] Basque rituals, like going to Basque hotels, are a "multi-layered channel of communication"[67] that foster the experience of "intense fantasies of belonging."[68] Food is a "home-making practice"[69] that re/creates a community where intergroup members are identified.

While the era of *Shoshone Mike* might suggest the already-mentioned cattle-versus-sheep conflict—"the economic dimensions of the competition for foraging . . . [in which] Basque sheepherders contended with white American cattlemen"[70]—it is also true that "in most areas settled cattlemen and sheepmen . . . managed a mutual accommodation."[71] An example of this mutual understanding is the case of Old Man Etcheverry, Mitch's grandfather, who has a ranch in California that his son, Sam, inherits when the former passes away. Not only does Old Man Etcheverry "[run]

---

61 *Wild Game*, 80.
62 Ibid.
63 *Jesse's Ghost*, 5.
64 Lisa M. Corcostegui, "Moving Emblems," in *The Basque Diaspora*, ed. William A. Douglass et al. (Reno: Basque Studies Program), 249.
65 Robyn Longhurst, Lynda T. Johnston, and Elsie Ho. "A Visceral Approach: Cooking 'at Home' with Migrant Women in Hamilton, New Zealand," *Transactions of the Institute of British Geographers* 34, no. 3 (2009), 334.
66 Ibid.
67 Mark Slobin, "Music in Diaspora," *Diaspora* 3 (Winter 1994), 244.
68 Martin Stokes, "Migrant/Migrating Music and the Mediterranean," in *Migrating Music*, eds. Jason Toynbee and Dueck B. Byron (New York: Routledge, 2011), 29.
69 Jayani Bonnerjee, Alison Blunt, Cathy McIlwaine, and Clifford Pereira, *Connected Communities* (Queen Mary University of London, 2012), 23.
70 Stephen Aron, *The American West* (New York: Oxford University Press, 2015), 76.
71 Lane and Douglass, *Basque Sheepherders*, 37.

sheep and cattle . . . in open pasture"[72] on his ranch, but he also hires cowboys to work for him. That is the case of Duane, who represents the Marlboro Man in the novel.[73] In fact, *Jesse's Ghost* offers another vivid manifestation of Basques merging into the mainstream and feeling both Basque and Westerners at the same time. Irigaray and Etcheverry embody this harmonious blend of Basqueness and westerness. While Irigaray retains the essence of the Old West within contemporary America, Etcheverry reflects the multicultural and multiethnic West, with its social and racial hierarchies of Okies, Mexicans, Armenians, Russians, Blacks, Bascos, and other communities that share the same geography. Indeed, as already suggested, many elements in Bergon's fiction are the outcome of his own firsthand experience. The choice to be a Basque and a westerner, and the way Bergon's childhood and teen years in the San Joaquin Valley shaped his identity reveal a multidimensional awareness and voluntary affiliation when constructing one's identity.

Jesse's Ghost explicitly confirms the fact that many immigrants were obliged to shorten or modify their Basque surnames to look more Anglo. This practice sometimes developed from a belief that it would help them to reduce conflict and misunderstandings. Often the immigration staff at Ellis Island was unable to decipher names and surnames accurately, which obliged many to simplify their first and last names. Similarly, this maneuver was thought to help newcomers assimilate faster into the mainstream. In the novel, Etcheverry and Sonny, who is the Okie narrator of *Jesse's Ghost*, go to a supermarket, Etchy's market, the Etcheverria's little grocery store. Etcheverry tells Sonny that he might have had the same surname as Etcheverria had some of his ancestors not changed it awhile back "to make it more American."[74] Etchy is talking "in Basco to a sheepherder from Nevada named Patxi Etxeberria Auertenetxea."[75] Etcheverry unveils that this is the real Basque spelling, with "tx" rather than "ch."[76] On the other hand, this scenario demonstrates, as discussed earlier, the fact that older generations are able to speak Basque and actually use it among themselves. Conversely, younger generations, who are prouder to be Basque, cannot speak it for the reasons discussed previously.

---

72   *Jesse's Ghost*, 133.
73   Ibid., 56.
74   Ibid., 73.
75   Ibid.
76   Euskaltzaindia, The Royal Academy of the Basque Language, dictates the use of "tx" as the spelling for the "ch" Spanish sound (https://www.euskaltzaindia.eus/en/).

To sum up, Bergon's four novels illustrate the horizontal and vertical relationships that encompass the experience of Basques in both the past and present West, while they also give us a hint of the future Basque American West. Bergon's novels trace the transformation of the term "Basco" as originally derogatory to the same term expressing Basque ethnic pride and recognition by the mainstream. As a matter of fact, Irigaray himself claims that he has grown "used to the nickname [Basco], although it had come about only in recent years."[77] Bergon is so far the only novelist who has orchestrated so linearly the rite of passage of the Basque American community from its establishment to the present. His careful selection of stories and characters inarguably mirrors the Basque world in the American West: how initially "[m]ost were not concerned with the survival of Basque culture; they were preoccupied with their own survival,"[78] and how this feeling then shifted into hybridizations to form a unique identity while simultaneously desiring to be part of a larger community.

Similarly, Bergon's Basque American figures are representations of the many ways to celebrate being Basque. Erramouspe, Arrizabalaga, Irigaray, and Etcheverry exemplify some possible choices for ethnic affiliation. While earlier generations tried to minimize the risk of being seen as different and to maximize their assimilation into American culture, to others today being Basque is a means to combat the monotony and the despair of everyday America.

Another possibility is to choose not to be Basque or not to publicly manifest it. Hence, as illustrated through the Basque world in Bergon's fiction, Basque ethnicity is historically variable, circumstantial, and situational, as well as voluntary.[79]

Finally, Bergon's novels present the opportunity to review the discriminating role adopted by many in the Basque Country as well as in America in defining who is/is not Basque and what it is to be Basque. While many, especially in the Basque Country, would claim that Erramouspe is more Basque than Irigaray, the truth is that Irigaray, along with the many contemporary Basques he represents, feels more Basque than Erramouspe. Rituals and norms are merely artificial devices that can be inclusive but can also often be exclusive and marginalizing. Certainly, " [c]ultural engineers' and elites who 'invent' traditions"[80] oblige individuals into involuntary or

77   *Wild Game*, 3.
78   Joe Eiguren. Interview Archived at the Basque Museum and Culture Center, Boise, Idaho.
79   Totoricagüena, *Identity, Culture, and Politics*, 200.
80   Sheffer, *Diaspora Politics*, 19.

"forced transformations"[81] through explicit rituals and unwritten norms. The resulting conceptual boundaries and classifications are adopted by policymakers who judge with authority and consequently color and prescribe the mainstream's approach to migrant and diasporic cross-borders and cross-identities. Questions such as "Does one necessarily have to be an 'active' Basque, or can one be a 'passive' Basque?"[82] demonstrate the urge to counterbalance core and peripheral practices. Social-spatial as well as chronological perspectives need to be borne in mind to permit natural and loyal individual and collective re/inventions. Erramouspe, Arrizabalaga, Irigaray, and Etcheverry cunningly mirror the various ways to feel and be Basque in the diaspora and in the homeland. Undoubtedly, Bergon's fiction broadens one's view of what it is to be and feel Basque.

WORKS CITED

Alba, Richard D. *Ethnic Identity: The Transformation of White America.* New Haven: Yale University Press, 1990.

Álvarez Gila, Oscar, and Iker Arranz Otaegui. "La Imagen del Inmigrante Vasco en El Cine: ¿Reflejo, Construcción o Refuerzo de los Estereotipos Sociales?." *Revista de Letras y Ficción Audiovisual* 4 (2014): 68-96.

Aron, Stephen. *The American West: A Very Short Introduction.* New York: Oxford University Press, 2015.

Bergon, Frank. *Shoshone Mike.* 1987. New York: Penguin Books, 1989.

———. *The Temptations of St. Ed & Brother S.* Reno: University of Nevada Press, 1993.

———. *Wild Game.* Reno: University of Nevada Press, 1995.

———. *Jesse's Ghost.* Berkeley: Heyday, 2011.

---

81 Grant McCracken, *Transformations* (Bloomington: Indiana University Press, 2008), 236.
82 Gloria Totoricagüena, *The Basques of New York* (2003; Reno: Center for Basque Studies, 2005), 333.

Bieter, John and Mark Bieter. *An Enduring Legacy: The Story of Basques in Idaho.* Reno: University of Nevada Press, 2000.

Bonnerjee, Jayani, Alison Blunt, Cathy McIlwaine, and Clifford Pereira. *Connected Communities: Diaspora and Transnationality.* Queen Mary University of London, 2012.

Brewer, Marilyn B. *Intergroup Relations.* Buckingham: Open University Press (1996), 2003. Camus Etchecopar, Argitxu. *The North American Basque Organizations (NABO), Incorporated/ Ipar Ameriketako Euskal Elkarteak, 1973-2007.* Gasteiz: Urazaindi Bilduma, Eusko Jaurlaritzaren Argitalpen Zerbitzu Nagusia, 2007.

Corcostegui, Lisa M. "Moving Emblems: Basque Dance and Symbolic Ethnicity." In *The Basque Diaspora/La Diáspora Vasca,* edited by William A. Douglass, Carmelo Urza, Linda White, and Joseba Zulaika. 249-273. Reno: Basque Studies Program, 1999.

Crawford, Kristina. "The Chains of Family: Basque Migration and the Archaeological Record." *California Archaeology* 4 (Spring 2012): 55–68.

Douglass, William A. "A World Eclipsed: Economic Changes Cause an Identity Crisis for Basque Americans." *The World and I: A Chronicle of Our Changing Era* (December 1993): 256-265.

Douglass, William A., and Jon Bilbao. *Amerikanuak: Basques in the New World.* Reno: University of Nevada Press, 1975.

Echeverria, Jeronima. *Home Away from Home: A History of Basque Boardinghouses.* Reno: University of Nevada Press, 1999.

Eiguren, Joe. Interview Archived at the Basque Museum and Culture Center, Boise, Idaho. Etulain, Richard W. *The Oregon Encyclopedia "Basques."* March 17, 2018. https://oregonencyclopedia.org/articles/basques/#.XEnzQ1xKjIU (accessed January 24, 2019).

———. *Basques of the Pacific Northwest.* Boise: University of Idaho Press, 1991.

———. "Basque Beginnings in the Pacific Northwest." *Idaho Yesterdays* 18 (Spring 1979): 26-32.

Euskaltzaindia. n.d. https://www.euskaltzaindia.eus/en/ (accessed January 23, 2019). Fernández de Larrinoa, Kepa. "The Western Basque Festival: Morfología y Contenido en La Invención de La Tradición." In *Los Otros Vascos: Las Migraciones Vascas en el Siglo XX,* edited by Xabier F. Medina, 105-127. Madrid: Editorial Fundamentos, 1997.

Garikano, Asun. *Far Westeko Euskal Herria.* Iruñea: Pamiela, 2009.

Hansen, Marcus L. *The Problem of the Third Generation Immigrant.* Rock Island: Augustana Historical Society, 1938.

Kelly, James P. *The Settlement of Basques in the American West.* Senior paper, Harvard University, 1967.

Lane, Richard H. and William A. Douglass. *Basque Sheepherders of the American West: A Photographic Documentary.* Reno: University of Nevada Press, 1985.

Lane, Richard H. "Trouble in the Sweet Promised Land: Basques in Early 20th Century Northeastern Nevada." In *Anglo-American Contributions to Basque Studies: Essays in Honor of Jon Bilbao,* edited by William A. Douglass, Richard W. Etulain, and William H. Jacobsen, Jr., 33-41. Reno: Desert Research Institute, 1977.

Laughlin, Mike. "Basque Ranching Culture in the Great Basin." *Northeastern Nevada Historical Society Quarterly* 3 & 4 (2010): 38-45.

Laxalt, Robert. *Sweet Promised Land.* Reno: University of Nevada Press (1957), 2007.

Limerick, Patricia N. *The Legacy of Conquest: The Unbroken Past of the American West.* New York: W W Norton and Company, Inc., 1987.

Longhurst, Robyn, Lynda T. Johnston, and Elsie Ho, "A Visceral Approach: Cooking 'at Home' with Migrant Women in Hamilton, New Zealand." *Transactions of the Institute of British Geographers* 34, no. 3 (2009): 333-345.

Luebke, Frederick C. "Introduction." In *European Immigrants in the American West: Community Histories,* edited by Frederick C. Luebke, vii-xix. Albuquerque: University of New Mexico Press, 1998.

Madinabeitia, Monika. "Getting to Know Frank Bergon: The Legacy of the Basque *Indarra.*" *Society of Basque Studies in America* 28 (2008): 69-75.

McCracken, Grant. *Transformations: Identity Constructions in Contemporary Culture.* Bloomington: Indiana University Press, 2008.

Oiarzabal, M. Agustín, and Pedro J. Oiarzabal. *La identidad vasca en el mundo: Narrativas sobre identidad más allá de las fronteras.* Bilbao: Erroteta, 2005.

Ray, Nina M., and John P. Bieter. " 'It Broadens Your View of Being Basque': Identity Through History, Branding and Cultural Policy." *International Journal of Cultural Policy* 21, no. 3 (2015): 1-17.

Saitua, Iker. *Basque Immigrants and Nevada's Sheep Industry: Geopolitics and the Making of an Agricultural Workforce, 1880-1954.* Reno: University of Nevada Press, 2019.

———. "The Best Sheepherder. The Racial Stereotype of Basque Immigrants in the American West Between the End of the Nineteenth and the Beginning of the Twentieth Centuries." *Historia Contemporánea* 56 (2018): 81-119. "VII Measurement of the Street Use of Languages: Basque Country, 2016." Soziolinguistika Klusterra, July 2017 (accessed August 5, 2019).

Sheffer, Gabriel. *Diaspora Politics.* 2003. Cambridge: Cambridge University Press, 2006.

Slobin, Mark. "Music in Diaspora: The View from Euro-America." *Diaspora* 3 (Winter 1994): 243-251.

Slotkin, Richard. *Regeneration Through Violence: The Mythology of the American Frontier, 1600-1860.* Hanover: Wesleyan University Press, 1973.

Sowards, Adam M. "What It Means to Be American." *Why Sheep Started So Many Wars in the American West.* October 5, 2017. http://www.whatitmeanstobeamerican. org/identities/why- sheep-started-so-many-wars-in-the-american-west/ (accessed January 23, 2019).

Stokes, Martin. "Migrant/Migrating Music and the Mediterranean." In *Migrating Music,* edited by Jason Toynbee and Dueck B. Byron, 28-37. New York: Routledge, 2011.

Taylor, Charles. "The Politics of Recognition." In *Multiculturalism and the Politics of Recognition,* edited by Amy Gutmann, 25-73. Princeton, NJ: Princeton University Press, 1994.

Totoricagüena Egurrola, Gloria P. "The Basque Language Abroad: Homeland and Diaspora Initiatives for Euskara." In *The Legal Status of the Basque Language Today,* edited by Gloria Totoricagüena Egurrola and Iñigo Urrutia Libarona, 43-72. Donostia: Eusko Ikaskuntza, 2008.

———. *Identity, Culture, and Politics in the Basque Diaspora.* Reno: University of Nevada Press, 2004.

———. *Basque Diaspora: Migration and Transnational Identity.* Reno: Center for Basque Studies, 2004.

———. *The Basques of New York: A Cosmopolitan Experience.* 2003. Reno: Center for Basque Studies, 2005.

————. "Euskonews." *Ethnic Industries for Migrants: Basque Sheepherding in the American West.* 2003. http://www.euskonews.eus/0212zbk/kosmo21201. html (January 23, 2019).

Frank Bergon's Western and Basque American Heroes: Deconstructing Archetypes

David Rio

Despite the extraordinary resilience of the myth of the West both in America and beyond the States, in the last few decades so-called post-western writing has favored an increasing demand for complex stories, breaking with the archetypal conflicts between good and evil and the predictable stock of characters in popular western fiction. These stories show their readers a complicated West, including, as Richard W. Etulain has claimed, "collisions and conflicts, alongside conversations, commitments, and even combinations."[1] The complexity of new western writing is illustrated, for example, by Frank Bergon's fiction, consisting of the novels *Shoshone Mike* (1987), *The Temptations of St. Ed & Brother S* (1993), *Wild Game* (1995), and *Jesse's Ghost* (2011). In this essay, I argue that Bergon's fiction departs from archetypal views of male heroes related to frontier mythology or to Basque idiosyncrasy and experiences in the American West. In fact, his novels challenge stereotypical portraits of the western hero, rejecting simplistic binary models and vindicating complex features in the configuration of their main protagonists. Particular attention will be paid to issues of masculine individualism, toughness, and physical strength and their problematic representation in Bergon's fiction, especially in connection with the foundational myths of the West and traditional male Basque patterns. Bergon's deconstruction of archetypal cowboy heroism, exposing its artificiality and ethnocentrism, not only offers a more realistic view of the American West, but it also contributes significantly to the increasing recognition and vitality of contemporary western American literature.

Since the publication of his first novel, *Shoshone Mike*, listed in 2001 among the top-twelve westerns by Oxford University Press's *Good Fiction*

1   I am indebted to the Basque Government (IT 1026-16) and to the Spanish Ministry of Education, Culture, and Sports (PGC2018- 094659-B- C21), FEDER for funding the research carried out for this essay. Richard Etulain, "Beyond Conflict, Toward Complexity: New Views of the American West," in *Exploring the American Literary West: International Perspectives*, ed. David Rio et al. (Bilbao: Universidad del País Vasco, 2006), 37.

Guide,[2] Frank Bergon has shown his gift for challenging stereotypical re-creations of the American West. As I have argued elsewhere, "*Shoshone Mike* illustrates the increasing de-heroification of post-frontier writing. The glorification of the archetypal western hero is replaced by a more realistic portrait of western types and by an ironic perspective of the myths prevailing in the West."[3] In this book, Bergon novelizes the so-called last Indian battle or last Indian massacre. Both names refer to a tragic incident in northwest Nevada in 1911 in which Shoshone Mike and part of his band were killed in revenge for the murder of four stockmen, three Basque shepherds and an Anglo cattleman. *Shoshone Mike* lacks a single central character because Bergon prefers to use a rotating point of view that allows him to approach the 1911 massacre from different perspectives and to offer an insightful psychological portrayal of some of its protagonists. The narrative focus of the story shifts among several characters, and this fragmentation serves Bergon by illustrating the variety of social and historical circumstances involved in this tragic event. The novel includes two main male characters, Shoshone Mike and Sheriff Lamb, but Bergon refuses to end his book with the archetypal confrontation of the formula western between the lawman and the renegade Indian in order not to distort historical facts. As Bergon has stated, "it would have been more dramatic to have the novel's main characters, Sheriff Lamb and Shoshone Mike, confront each other in the final battle, but such an encounter did not occur."[4]

In his depiction of Sheriff Lamb in the novel, Frank Bergon has constructed a character reflective of the evolution of the classic western protagonist. Bergon's sheriff does not conform to the paradigm of the western folk hero, a character who often embodies archetypal traits of vigilante justice in frontier mythology. Although in his stoicism and laconism Lamb may resemble some iconic images of the sheriff in traditional westerns, he is not a lonesome, all-powerful figure who is forced to resort to violence to resolve problems and purge society of lawless vandals.

Instead, he is a society-oriented lawman who does not fit into the features of the lone, just man as hero and whose commitment to protect

---

2   Edited by Jane Rogers et al. (New York), 136. The list included, among others, Stephen Crane's "The Bride Comes to Yellow Sky" (1898), Owen Wister's *The Virginian* (1902), Walter Van Tilburg Clark's *The Ox-Bow Incident* (1940), E.L. Doctorow's *Welcome to Hard Times* (1960), and Larry McMurtry's *Lonesome Dove* (1985).

3   David Rio, "Exploring the Basque Legacy in Frank Bergon's Fiction," in *Exploring the American Literary West: International Perspectives*, 207.

4   David Rio, "Basques in the International West: An Interview with Frank Bergon," *Western American Literature* 21, no. 1 (Spring 2001): 61–62

the community is undermined both by his own doubts about how to face savagery and by his distrust of violence to restore social order. Lamb is the real name of the Winnemucca sheriff who had to deal with the "last Indian massacre," though its allegorical connotations are obvious, too. Bergon uses Lamb as a symbol of the problematic transition from the codes of the Old West, where revenge often replaces the power of the law, to a New West, where reflective justice is given priority over the hero's violent destruction of the lawbreakers. Lamb is not a solitary sheriff, but a man with a family, troubled with several marital issues that somehow weaken his position as a lawman. This domestic context places Lamb close to other western heroes whose marital status intrudes on their duties as lawmen, such as Sheriff Potter in Stephen Crane's remarkable story "The Bride Comes to Yellow Sky" (1898) or Sheriff Kane in *High Noon* (1952). Bergon's portrayal of Sheriff Lamb explores a version of masculinity that departs from classic western archetypes of the hero. Instead of emphasizing individual masculine force as a dominant trait in a genre that, as Jane Tompkins has observed, "worships the phallus,"[5] Bergon creates a lawman whose idea of masculinity is linked to a strong sense of responsibility for those weaker than him. Lamb does not epitomize traditional masculine features in frontier mythology, such as individuality, dominance, physical strength, and gunmanship, though it is known that in the past he has been forced to kill a man. He seems closer to more realistic reconfigurations of masculinity where vulnerability, patience, and doubts become important ingredients in the hero's personality. Lamb is depicted as a troubled protagonist who not only faces spiritual confusion, but who is also unable to fulfill the expectations of the community for its sheriff. Whereas in classical westerns, as John G. Cawelti has argued, "the hero's special skill at gunfighting not only symbolizes his masculine potency, but indicates that his violence is disciplined and pure,"[6] in *Shoshone Mike* Sheriff Lamb's relationship with violence is quite frustrating because he is unable to stop the posse from taking the law into its own hands. Through Lamb's limitations as a hero and his moral and spiritual dilemmas, Bergon offers an insightful revisionist interpretation of the western lawman, portraying a West in transition where frontier mythology intertwines with New West realities.

---

5   Jane Tompkins, *West of Everything: The Inner Life of Westerns* (Oxford: Oxford University Press, 1992), 28.

6   John Cawelti, *The Six-Gun Mystique* (Bowling Green, OH: Bowling Green University Popular Press, 1971), 60.

In *Shoshone Mike*, Bergon does not limit his scope to deconstructing the classical lawman archetype; he also debunks the stereotypical image of another major character in the western, the savage. Although there is no common agreement about the different variations of the image of Native Americans in traditional western stories, and some scholars mention the existence of seven Indian stereotypes[7] and others even talk about ten,[8] most authors emphasize two dominant images: the noble Indian and the bloodthirsty savage. Michael Hilger, for example, has explained that "even such great directors as D. W. Griffith and John Ford portray the Indian as always too good or too bad; as such they are often the most extreme fictions in the western, a genre that seldom comes very close to reality."[9] Bergon is aware of the weight of these two stereotypes in the western tradition, but in his portrayal of Shoshone Mike he refuses to identify him with any of these recurrent images, giving priority to realism, complexity, and individuation over widespread ethnocentric representations of Native Americans in classical westerns. Bergon's rejection of simplistic images in his characterization of Shoshone Mike is even illustrated by the title of the novel, a hybrid moniker that, as the author himself has pointed out, "thematically symbolizes his divided existence between a traditional Native American world and a modern Anglo one."[10] The novel stresses the conflict between reality (Shoshone Mike is an old, harmless Indian with a record of peaceful coexistence with white people) and myth (the archetypal view of the Native American as a dangerous renegade who should be exterminated because it means a threat to progress).

Bergon exposes the dangers of stereotypes in frontier mythology because of their power to promote spaces of exclusion that, for example, in the case of the Native Americans relegate them to a nonhuman condition. As Willard F. Enteman has noted, "a stereotype's goal is converting real persons into artificial persons. In our stereotypical acts, we ignore the individuality of people and treat them as proxies for some group we have decided they should represent. . . . In short, we deny them their humanity."[11] Similarly, David Sibley has claimed that "to animalize or dehumanize a

---

7   See Mary Alice Money, "Broken Arrows: Images of Native Americans in the Popular Western," in *American Indian Studies: An Interdisciplinary Approach to Contemporary Issues*, ed. by Dane Morrison (New York: Peter Lang, 1997), 363–388.

8   See Rick Hill, "High-Speed Film Captures the Vanishing American, in Living Color," *American Indian Culture and Research Journal* 20, no. 3 (1996): 111–128.

9   Michael Hilger, *The American Indian in Film* (Lanham, MD: Scarecrow Press, 1986), 1.

10   Rio, "Interview with Frank Bergon," 62–63.

11   Willard F. Enteman, "Stereotyping, Prejudice, and Discrimination," in *Images That Injure: Pictorial Stereotypes in the Media*, ed. Paul Martin Lester (Westport, CT: Greenwood, 1996), 10.

minority group [. . .] legitimates persecution."[12] In *Shoshone Mike*, the Native Americans are presented by the local newspapers as "real savages, unmixed of blood, who had carried into these days of civilization all the savagery of the days before the white man's coming."[13] In fact, Shoshone Mike and his band are regarded not only as an obstacle for progress, but also as a threat to the way of life of the white man: "as long as they were free to move about, no man in all that wide country might feel safe to leave his ranch or to follow his occupation."[14] Bergon counterbalances this construction of Shoshone Mike and his people as the Other who symbolizes lawlessness, rejection of the town, and ruthless violence, with the emphasis on their former peaceful coexistence with white ranchers in Nevada and Idaho. Certainly, Shoshone Mike and his family are reluctant to interact with the white world, but this attitude is justified by their wish to remain loyal to an ancient lifestyle. Besides, Shoshone Mike is not depicted by Bergon as an outlaw loner, but as a family man concerned about the survival of his relatives, whose decision to resort to violence should be regarded mainly as an act of misguided revenge. Overall, although the survival of the bloodthirsty savage stereotype plays an important role in the violent episodes described in the novel; violence is not presented as the inevitable result of the conflict between two different cultures, but as the consequence of several tragic misunderstandings. Bergon himself has underscored that "the massacre didn't have to happen. If the massacre had been inevitable, it wouldn't have been tragic. [. . .] Tragedy is the consequence of choices. Other choices might have been made."[15]

The use of a rotating point of view allows Bergon to include in *Shoshone Mike* other male characters who embody different variations of the hero archetype. Thus, some characters, such as Captain Donnelley of the Nevada State Police or Mort West, a young member of the posse, seem to cling to the foundational myths of the West as a constitutive part of their male identity. Donnelley, the leader of the vengeful posse, may certainly be defined as a paradoxical character because he defends Wild West rules and, in particular revenge, in the name of progress. Mort West, for his part, pursues the fantasy of becoming a hero in the old western tradition and the posse means for him, above all, a test of manhood and acceptance. As a contrast, we also find two male characters in the novel

---

12   David, Sibley, *Geographies of Exclusion: Society and Difference in the West* (London: Routledge, 1995), 10.
13   Frank Bergon, *Shoshone Mike* (New York: Viking, 1987), 256.
14   Ibid.
15   Rio, "Interview with Frank Bergon," 62.

who depart from archetypal masculinity ideals of the wild western hero. One of them is the Winnemucca pastor, Father Enright, a tormented and confused priest unable to stop the savage revenge of his white community. He is aware both of his failure to bring civilization with his sermons instead of a gun and of the hazy line separating the savage from the civilized in the American West of the first decades of the twentieth century: "We said they were savages. We said they were going to destroy our homes, our families, our laws, everything that made us people. [. . .] We did to them exactly what we said they were going to do to us. What does that make us?"[16] Another interesting character is Jean Erramouspe, the son of one of the Basque sheepherders killed by Shoshone Mike. He symbolizes the discrimination and prejudice toward Basque immigrants in the American West, but his portrayal cannot be regarded as one-dimensional in terms of his ethnicity. Certainly, toughness and endurance are important ingredients of his personality, and his admiration for his father's physical strength seems to link Jean to classical representations of Basque masculinity in which fortitude and forbearance become key traits, often summed up in the Basque term *indarra*. However, this character does not fit into archetypal images of Basque men acting submissively in relation to women in their families, as shown in his rebellion against his female relatives' attempts to prevent him from participation in the posse: "Am I supposed to sit here while everyone else gets revenge except me?"[17] However, the novel reveals that Jean does not fit either into the classical western male archetype of the avenger who seeks revenge against someone who has wronged him. The reader may witness his spiritual growth from his initial wish to participate in the posse to his awareness of the futility of this revenge and the acceptance of his father's death as the consequence of a tragic misunderstanding related to the resilience of old western cultural stereotypes. In the end, the posse becomes for him a charade because, as he claims, "there were no heroes; the whole thing was stupid, mishandled."[18]

Bergon's second novel, *The Temptations of St. Ed & Brother S* does not deconstruct traditional western heroism, because the novel is not set in the Old West, but the book offers an interesting revision of archetypal models of male protagonists, emphasizing complexity and integration of polarities. The novel, set in the nuclear age, centers on two monks (St. Ed and Brother S), whose labor at the Hermitage of Solitude on the edge of the Nevada Test Site is threatened by federal plans to build a nuclear

16   *Shoshone Mike*, 269.
17   Ibid., 170.
18   Ibid., 263.

waste disposal at a nearby mountain.[19] The novel focuses on both male protagonists and, although there are important differences between them, the novel cannot be reduced to a simplistic binary opposition between both religious figures. In fact, Bergon once again rejects one-dimensional approaches in the configuration of his main characters and stresses their internal contradictions and their complex, hybrid features. For example, in his depiction of St. Ed (Father Edward St. John Arrizabalaga), Bergon chooses not to represent a flat character, based on the ascetic archetype, underscoring instead the blending of multiple traits in his personality and the integration of conflicting features. His own name illustrates some of these complex characteristics, such as his mixed ancestry (he is half-Basque[20] and half-English) or the precarious balance between his devotion to spirituality and his earlier mundane way of life. As we may read in the novel, the name "St. Ed" was "a joke among seminarians because of his previous marriage and worldly experience."[21] Even geographic polarities seem to merge in this character because he was born in Boston but he is committed to build a new monastic order in the Nevada desert. Eclecticism extends to his formal religious duty because he is both a priest (he is the pastor of St. Anthony's parish) and a monk (the abbot of the Hermitage of Solitude in the Desert). Also, if we examine St. Ed's role in the novel in connection to traditional frontier mythology, we may observe that he represents a double and contradictory western dimension. On the one hand, his commitment to open a monastery in the desert places him close to prototypical images of the pioneers in the West. On the other hand, his refusal to conform to the federal government's plans to build a nuclear waste repository connects him with the Native Americans in the area who regard the desert as a living and sacred earth. In fact, both groups, the monks and the Native Americans, are regarded by the U.S. Department of Energy as an obstacle to progress. St. Ed's complex personality is also illustrated by his double language (he combines religious sermons with profanity and rude expressions) and, above all, by his confusion about his relationship with the world existing beyond his hermitage. His devotion to old monastic practices symbolized by his retreat in the desert hermitage seems to place him away from the controversy about nuclear waste disposal. However,

---

19　The novel is not based on actual events, but it evokes the increasing opposition in Nevada to the federal government's proposal for a nuclear repository at Yucca Mountain.

20　As Frank Bergon has noted, St. Ed's Basqueness "aggrandizes his personal sense of individuality, specialness, and even uniqueness" (Rio, "Interview with Frank Bergon," 64).

21　Frank Bergon, *The Temptations of St. Ed & Brother S* (Reno: University of Nevada Press, 1993), 6.

he cannot avoid his immersion into the profane world, as symbolized by his participation in a Las Vegas talk show to advertise his hermitage or by his final decision to take an active role in the nuclear controversy. After all, he realizes that both spiritual matters and material issues are intertwined: "there is only one world. Not a profane world over here and a sacred world over there."[22] This integration of apparently opposite elements is also epitomized by what we might call a troubled masculinity. As a matter of fact, in St. Ed's life, restraint and commitment to self-imposed religious discipline, including celibacy, coexist uneasily with the temptations of the world, represented by sex, bad temper, and boxing.

Bergon's portrayal of the second religious male protagonist of his novel, Brother S, also contains a revision of standard models of behavior related to masculinity and to archetypal American attitudes. Bergon emphasizes Brother S's refusal to conform to traditional male interests exemplified by "girlfriends, parties, sports, cars, booze,"[23] and also his rejection of standard American social patterns: "he didn't want to return to the world to get married, get a job, buy a house, raise kids, watch TV, and drift along the predictable currents of the American Dream."[24] His uniqueness is linked to his idealism and his longing for a mystical experience, and he seems to believe that self-alienation and self-sacrifice ("he wanted to know the strictest place the priest had ever heard of")[25] seem to be the right paths for spiritual fulfillment. Ironically enough, Brother S's search for a unique way of life and his isolationist attitude place him very close to stereotypical independent western characters, and in a way his devotion to an eremitic, simple, primitive way of life may be regarded as the incarnation of the individualistic western spirit. The tension between uniqueness and the reproduction of western archetypes may also be observed in Brother S's decision to return to the world. He becomes a peculiar disc jockey in Las Vegas ("The Pharaoh of Love") and takes an active role in the fight against the nuclear repository. Like many heroes in classical westerns, this character is forced to replace passivity by action, rejecting his original isolationist beliefs: "The world always followed you into your retreat. The only thing to do against such evil was to strike back."[26] Brother S's uniqueness becomes problematic too if we examine his death. In fact, his shooting by the security troops at the nuclear test site seems to re-create

---

22   Ibid., 305.
23   Ibid., 4.
24   Ibid.
25   Ibid., 6.
26   Ibid., 291

the archetypal sacrifice of the individual western hero for the well-being of the community. Bergon once again resorts to classical images in frontier mythology, though he integrates them into different contexts and adds new perspectives that enhance the complexity of his characters. We may even see that, at the end of the novel, Brother S's death seems to become the catalyst of a new temptation for these monks, to turn Brother S into a martyr and his death into a heroic deed that may contribute to the genesis of a new hermitage.

In his third novel, *Wild Game*, Bergon seems to return to the historical novelist genre, but this time he employs a relatively recent western event as the main center of his story: the fifteenth-month manhunt for survivalist and convicted killer Claude Dallas in the 1980s. Dallas murdered two Idaho State fish-and-game wardens in the Owyhee Desert near the Nevada border and after his arrest became a controversial figure in the American West. Whereas some supported Dallas as the quintessential western free man, others regarded him simply as a cold-blooded murderer.

Bergon's fictional approach to this episode should be linked, as Gregory L. Morris has noted, to his interest in exploring the "profound relationship between what might be called the 'manufactured West' and the competing western visions that seek to redefine the West."[27] In fact, the tension between the myth of the West and the realities of the New West is one of the main themes of the novel. Bergon chooses a biologist for the Nevada Division of Wildlife, Jack Irigaray, as the main protagonist of his narrative. This character epitomizes new western values and attitudes, in particular, the protection of the environment, and he also represents modern definitions of masculinity and strength. His commitment to the defense of the natural ecosystem and his love of the wilderness are not connected to mythic masculine models based on the justification of violence to maintain the law. He even rejects the archetypal opposition between human law and natural law, arguing that in nature "for the most part, peaceful coexistence was the real law. Predators don't fight each other. In fact, the survival of the fittest rested on the avoidance of fighting."[28] This new version of the western masculine, self-epitomized by Irigaray, is not only restricted to the natural world, but is also noticeable in the domestic space. Thus, Bergon shows us Irigaray's willingness to face his marital problems in a civilized way, even if his own sister accuses him of being too passive

---

27 Gregory L. Morris, *Frank Bergon*. Western Writers Series, 126 (Boise, ID: Boise State University, 1997), 38.
28 Frank Bergon, *Wild Game* (Reno: University of Nevada Press, 1995), 119.

with his wife. Similarly, we know about his concern and involvement in the education of his daughters, departing from traditional images dissociating western masculinity from domesticity. However, once again Bergon rejects offering a one-dimensional version of his main character and stresses his complex features, in particular, the inner tension between his new western ideals and his attraction toward frontier mythology. Irigaray feels tempted by traditional concepts associated with masculinity in the West, such a toughness, independence, individual mastery, or revenge as a duty. He is certainly influenced by iconic images of the West from a masculinist perspective and by culturally accepted traits of the western hero. In fact, Bergon establishes an interesting comparison between Irigaray and his enemy in the novel, Billy Crockett, the fictional counterpart of Claude Dallas. Although the whole novel is based on the opposition of these two varieties of westerners (in particular, due to their different attitudes to the western landscape), it may be argued that there is also a male bond between Irigaray and Crockett, as it happens in many classical westerns. As Jane Tompkins has explained, in popular westerns "the hero frequently forms a bond with another man—sometimes his rival, more often a comrade—a bond than is more important than any relationship he has with a woman and is frequently tinged with homoeroticism."[29] In *Wild Game*, it is hinted that Irigaray and Crockett share not only a clear physical resemblance, but also a common immersion into the male ethic of the West. Although Irigaray does not share Crockett's admiration for Louis L'Amour's novels, he cannot deny the influence of some of the values and prescriptions of the mythic West on his life. For example, he admits that "once, he had envied Billy's dream. As a boy, he'd lived for the thrill of being in open country."[30] Irigaray's problematic relationship with the archetypal image of the western hero is also influenced by his Basque heritage. His Basqueness, as Bergon himself has noted, "introduces Old World values and attitudes about revenge, toughness, and independence—or rather the protagonist's conception of those values—that are very close to those of the outlaw and which the protagonist must struggle to understand and overcome."[31] As a matter of fact, one of the most remarkable parts of the novel is Irigaray's inner struggle to avoid behaving like the outlaw (he will even try to hunt in Mexico in order to kill him) and his final rejection of the temptation of revenge. With Irigaray Bergon shows once again his distrust toward classical notions of the hero. It may be argued that this novel is another

---

29   Tompkins, *West of Everything*, 39.
30   Ibid., 122.
31   Rio, "Interview with Frank Bergon," 67.

example of Bergon's preference for complex protagonists who fail to achieve the attributes traditionally attached to one-dimensional heroes. As Monika Madinabeitia has observed, "the characters who manifest the need to scratch heroic perfection portray neither the image of confidence, nor the self-control, the strength and prowess that we expect from them."[32]

In *Wild Game*, Bergon's portrayal of the outlaw seems to be modeled on the archetypal features of the savage in traditional westerns. As John Cawelti has noted, Indians and outlaws share the same basic qualities in the popular western: "negatively, lawlessness, a love of violence, rejections of the town and its way of life and, more positively, the capacity to live and move freely in the wilderness, mastery of the tools of violence, and strong masculinity."[33] Thus, Billy Crockett is depicted as a poacher devoted to "natural laws" and opposed to "artificial laws," such as gaming laws ("this country is nothing but a dictatorship").[34] Through his devotion to a "natural" way of life he seems to re-create the myth of the frontier and, in particular, the figure of the "white Indian" or the free trapper, and to justify the use of violence: "life without bloodshed is impossible. We are all predators."[35] His name certainly echoes the Wild West days, as exemplified by Billy the Kid and Davy Crockett, and even his new alias, "Jack Atxaga," has symbolic connotations because it connects him to the hero of the novel, combining Irigaray's name with another Basque surname. Despite the obvious ethnic differences between Irigaray and Crockett, this alias is useful to tie Crockett to traditional Basque values of stubbornness, individualism, and toughness. Significantly enough, one of Crockett's main supporters is also a Basque, Jenny Zubillaga, in what seems to be another example of Bergon's interest in emphasizing the connection between old western mythology and archetypal Basque idiosyncrasy.[36]

Although in *Wild Game* Billy Crockett seems to embody the paradigm of the western folk hero, idealized by some local people and the media, Bergon deconstructs this character, revealing his complex personality. In fact, the novel shows that Crockett is neither a true westerner (he was born

---

32 Monika Madinabeitia, "Frank Bergon's Fiction: Complexity, Polarization, Diversity," in *Exploring the American Literary West: International Perspectives*, ed. David Rio et al. (Bilbao: Universidad del País Vasco, 2006), 218.

33 Cawelti, *Six-Gun Mystique*, 53–54.

34 *Wild Game*, 129.

35 Ibid., 2.

36 As I have argued elsewhere, the presence of a Basque American character as one of the main supporters of the villain of the novel may be regarded "as an attempt by Bergon to avoid ethnic chauvinism and to emphasize instead Basque heterogeneity" ("Exploring the Basque Legacy in Frank Bergon's Fiction," in *Exploring the American Literary West: International Perspectives*, 209).

and raised in Illinois) nor a mountain man. His abilities as a trapper or as hunter are questionable, and it is obvious that he is unable to understand animals ("he liked killing just to kill").[37] Even his toughness is rather artificial, and we may see him, for example, buying dental floss or health food. In Bergon's words, "he's mean, but not tough."[38] His idealization as a tough lonely frontier man by a TV movie and popular magazines clashes with the truth about his life. Although his acquittal in his last trial seems to prove the power of artificial archetypes ("image is all that counts"),[39] the doubts about his hero status are undeniable, as illustrated by the media coverage of his capture while buying groceries in a store in a suburb of Los Angeles: "JUST HOW TOUGH IS BILLY CROCKETT? SOME ARGUE IT WAS FRIENDS, NOT SKILLS, THAT KEPT HIM FREE.[40] [. . .] Do we have a true western hero left anywhere?"[41] After all, Billy Crockett exemplifies the public need to create heroes regardless of their real values or attitudes, which are subordinated to the power of the image. As Monika Madinabeitia has claimed, in Bergon's fiction "heroes emerge from the human need to create models to follow and to venerate,[. . .] heroes that are mainly human creations, rather than tangible beings."[42]

With *Wild Game* Bergon puts an end to his Nevada trilogy, but not to his interest in revising archetypal views of male heroes, as may be seen, for example, in *Jesse's Ghost*, the first volume of his new California trilogy.[43] This novel is inspired by real events, by Bergon's experiences growing up in the Central Valley, and it explores the dark side of rural California life. In fact, Gerald Haslam has pointed out that the novel might be called "rural noir."[44] The book focuses on memories of a second-generation tough "Okie," Sonny Childers, the narrator of the novel, whose adult life is haunted by a murder he committed years ago. The victim was his best friend, Jesse Floyd, with whom he shared a similar ethnic and social background. As is common in Bergon's previous novels, there are several references to Basque characters and elements, but this time the two protagonists are Scots-Irish descendants of the Dust Bowl "Okies." Sonny and Jesse also have an identity based on classical male iconography in common: girls,

---

37   Ibid., 92.
38   Rio, "Interview with Frank Bergon," 66.
39   *Wild Game*, 319.
40   Capital letters in the original text.
41   *Wild Game*, 301.
42   Madinabeitia, "Frank Bergon's Fiction," 218.
43   The second volume of this trilogy is a collection of essays, *Two-Buck Chuck & The Marlboro Man: The New Old West*, (Reno: University of Nevada Press, 2019).
44   Gerald Haslam, *Jesse's Ghost* (review), *Western American Literature* 47, no. 1 (Spring 2012): 94.

friends, drinks, cars, and, in particular, fights. Bergon explores a world where physical violence plays a key role, even as educational practice, as stated by the narrator of the novel: "our dads beat the hell out of all of us, and our mommas did, too, until we got too big."[45] Fighting in this novel works as ritualized violence and becomes both a powerful common bond for the main characters ("from then on I fought alongside him or watched him fight"),[46] and a source of pleasure ("Jesse just loved to fight. You can't ignore the pleasure of it").[47] Jesse and Sonny seem to reproduce traditional stereotypes about masculine identity in frontier mythology, with their overemphasis on toughness, dominance, and endurance. As Tara Rae Miner has stated, "their clichéd notions about manhood are classically western—the belief that in a land of seemingly limitless resources all it takes is hard work, toughness and a little luck to succeed."[48]

In this story of friendship and conflict, where even the narrator finds it problematic to define his relationship with Jesse ("I didn't hate Jesse . . . I loved him—or hated him because I loved him"),[49] Bergon stresses the power of this character to attract the love and often the admiration of other characters. As the narrator observes: "everybody liked Jesse. Adults, colored people, girls."[50] His success is a combination of physical features and spiritual traits ("he had those crystal clear blue eyes, a great smile, he was a hard worker and a loyal friend")[51] that turn Jesse into a folk hero. Most of his social and personal identity is based on his toughness, and fighting becomes for Jesse an instrument for survival, for recognition, or simply to prove himself.

However, the novel also exposes Jesse's reality behind his tough image and his appeal as a popular hero. For example, we learn that the toughest kid in the valley is afraid of spiders or that his popularity cannot help him to face social prejudice. In fact, he will be unable to marry Sonia because of his low social status. After all, he is just a dirt-poor "Okie" who in his mature years will even lose the pleasure of fighting, becoming ironically a target for others who long to destroy the myth of Jesse Floyd: "guys all

---

45   Frank Bergon, *Jesse's Ghost* (Berkeley, CA: Heyday, 2011), 11.
46   Ibid., 8.
47   Ibid., 35.
48   Tae Rae Miner, "To Die Fighting: A Review of *Jesse's Ghost: A Novel,*" *High Country News* (October 31, 2011). https://www.hcn.org/issues/43.18/to-die-fighting-a-review-of-jesses-ghost-a-novel (accessed January 9, 2019).
49   *Jesse's Ghost*, 39.
50   Ibid., 21.
51   Ibid., 24.

over the valley wanted to fight him for no reason at all, just because he was Jesse Floyd."[52]

As happened in previous novels, in *Jesse's Ghost* Bergon does not focus only on one male protagonist (Jesse), but he also allows his narrator (Sonny Childers) to play an important role in the story. We may define *Jesse's Ghost* as a novel with a double protagonist, though rather than talking about the presence of two heroes in this book, it would be more appropriate to define both Sonny and Jesse as anti-heroes. Bergon juxtaposes Sonny to Jesse, presenting him as a loser, confined to a subordinate male role due to Jesse's overwhelming shadow. Despite their similar blue-collar status and their common devotion to fighting ("there's no better feeling than kicking the shit out of somebody"),[53] it is obvious that Sonny cannot achieve Jesse's popularity. In fact, he often has to accept that he is only second choice to his friend, as illustrated by his first wife, who ends up complaining about "marrying a fucking wino loser."[54] The novel also reveals the declining weight of fighting in Sonny's identity during his mature years. His early love for the nobility of spontaneous fighting ("the art of war")[55] will disappear, and he will have to resort to an artificial surrogate, wrestling at a gym, to maintain some kind of connection with his archetypal ideals of manhood. His hurt pride, after learning about his wife being unfaithful to him with Jesse, will be the main reason for his killing his best friend while under the influence of alcohol. Despite this ultimate and tragic violent event, his inability to find peace after Jesse's murder and his determination to start a new life with a strong presence of religion ("no matter how many times a man sinks, there's a chance for redemption") also illustrate his rejection of the macho culture he had embraced in his earlier days. Both Jesse and Sonny epitomize Bergon's preference for well-rounded heroes who may apparently adhere to archetypal codes of conduct, but who increase in complexity and realism throughout the story.

Overall, Bergon's novels symbolize the increasing maturation of western American fiction and, in particular, the revision of the traditional overemphasis on individualistic male cultural models. With its departure from archetypal views of male heroes related to mythical views of the West or to particular ethnic groups, such as the Basques, Bergon's fiction reveals the existence of complex and changing definitions of masculinity and strength in the New West. Bergon's deconstruction of archetypal

---

52   Ibid., 170.
53   Ibid., 35.
54   Ibid., 174.
55   Ibid., 8.

cowboy heroism, exposing its artificiality, its ethnocentrism, and its simplistic dimension not only offers a more realistic view of the American West, but also contributes significantly to the growing recognition and vitality of contemporary western American literature.

WORKS CITED

Bergon, Frank. *Jesse's Ghost*. Berkeley, CA: Heyday, 2011.

——. *Shoshone Mike*. New York: Viking, 1987

——. *The Temptations of St. Ed & Brother S*. Reno: University of Nevada Press, 1993.

——. *Two-Buck Chuck & the Marlboro Man: The New Old West*. Reno: University of Nevada Press, 2019.

——. *Wild Game*. Reno: University of Nevada Press, 1995.

Cawelti, John G. *The Six-Gun Mystique*. Bowling Green, OH: Bowling Green University Popular Press, 1971.

Crane, Stephen. "The Bride Comes to Yellow Sky." *McClure's Magazine* (February 1898): 377–384.

Enteman, Willard F. "Stereotyping, Prejudice, and Discrimination." In *Images That Injure: Pictorial Stereotypes in the Media*, ed. by Paul Martin Lester, 15–22. Westport, CT: Greenwood, 1996.

Etulain, Richard W. "Beyond Conflict, Toward Complexity: New Views of the American West." In *Exploring the American Literary West: International Perspectives*, edited by David Rio et al., 25–38. Bilbao: Universidad del País Vasco, 2006.

Haslam, Gerald. *Jesse's Ghost* (review). *Western American Literature* 47, no. 1 (Spring 2012): 94.

Hilger, Michael. *The American Indian in Film*. Lanham, MD: Scarecrow Press, 1986.

Hill, Rick. "High-Speed Film Captures the Vanishing American, in Living Color." *American Indian Culture and Research Journal* 20, no. 3 (1996): 11–128.

Kramer, Stanley, et al. 1952. *High Noon*. Los Angeles, CA: United Artists.

Madinabeitia, Monika. "Frank Bergon's Fiction: Complexity, Polarization, Diversity." In *Exploring the American Literary West: International Perspectives*, ed. David Rio et al., 213–219. Bilbao: Universidad del País Vasco, 2006.

Miner, Tara Rae. "To Die Fighting: A Review of *Jesse's Ghost: A Novel*," *High Country News* (Oct. 31, 2011). https://www.hcn.org/issues/43.18/to-die-fighting-a-review-of-jesses-ghost-a-novel (accessed January 9, 2019).

Money, Mary Alice. "Broken Arrows: Images of Native Americans in the Popular Western." In *American Indian Studies: An Interdisciplinary Approach to Contemporary Issues*, ed. by Dane Morrison, 363–388. New York: Peter Lang, 1997.

Morris, Gregory L. *Frank Bergon*. Western Writers Series, 126. Boise: Boise State University, 1997.

Rio, David. "Basques in the International West: An Interview with Frank Bergon." *Western American Literature* 21.1 (Spring 2001): 56–72.

———. "Exploring the Basque Legacy in Frank Bergon's Fiction." In *Exploring the American Literary West: International Perspectives*, edited by David Rio et al., 203-212. Bilbao: Universidad del País Vasco, 2006.

Rogers, Jane, ed. *Good Fiction Guide*. New York; Oxford University Press, 2001.

Sibley, David. *Geographies of Exclusion: Society and Difference in the West*. London: Routledge, 1995.

Tompkins, Jane. *West of Everything: The Inner Life of Westerns*. Oxford: Oxford University Press, 1992

The Real Thing: Authenticity in Frank Bergon's Fiction

William Heath

First, full disclosure: I have been a close friend of Frank Bergon since we were colleagues at Vassar College in the 1970s. I have read each of his novels in manuscript and offered constructive criticism, mostly suggestions about how to tighten sentences and sharpen drama. He has done the same for my manuscripts. That we hold each other's work in high regard is a part of our friendship. Thus it is true that I have a bias in his favor, but as a fellow novelist and a literary critic, I trust that the following will shed light on the merits of his works.

Frank and I share some assumptions about the craft and purpose of fiction. My first novel, *The Children Bob Moses Led*, has a line from a Robert Penn Warren poem as its epigraph: "The world is real. It is there."[1] In our discussions of the contemporary literary scene, we often lament that popular fiction, and too many acclaimed novels, are formulaic fantasies whose purpose is to escape from, not engage with, the real world. What is often lacking is an author who actually knows what he or she is talking about, who speaks with authority about people living in a specific time and place—characters whose thoughts, words, and actions tell us something important about being human.

Nowadays, I realize, it is out of fashion to suggest that some authors know more than others and speak with an authority that convinces us of the authenticity of their fictive worlds. Granting that the interpretations of this essay are suspect in some critical circles, let me cite John Dewey's comment that often philosophy does not solve problems, it gets over them. Thus I plan to proceed as if Frank Bergon the author really exists,

---

1   Robert Penn Warren, "Court-Martial," *Selected Poems: New and Old 1923-1966* (New York: Random House, 1966), 164. Locating what is "real" can be problematic. In Bergon's fictions fact and myth can clash or merge. Like "the truth," reality can be elusive, but that's not to say everything is *absolutely* relative and there is no "there" there.

knows what he's talking about, and as if his novels engage us in worlds, set in the past or present, that matter.

Shoshone Mike

The origins of the novel trace back to Frank's Basque grandmother's house in Battle Mountain, Nevada, where as a child he heard tales of "the last Indian battle in America," the 1911 massacre of Shoshone Mike's small renegade band by a posse. Years later he was offended by an account, "more fantasy than fact," and he set out to correct the historical record.[2] His research—which extended beyond archives to interviews with the last two survivors, one white, one Shoshone—convinced him that he should write a novel. "I had the facts but not the truth," he realized, and only a work of fiction could dramatize the emotions at the heart of a "larger, over-arching Nevada story."[3] He invented a few figures, most notably Jean Erramouspe, yet the greatest challenge was to create credible voices, feelings, motivations, and actions for all of the characters. As Frank has noted, verification is the task of the historian, the novelist must master verisimilitude, a "semblance of life" that we can believe in and take seriously.[4]

Shoshone Mike is a moving ironic coda to the epic "winning" of the West. This first novel is a work of reflective maturity, marked by an inclusive moral vision, a firm grasp of the material, and an artistic control as unobtrusive as it is sure. The secret of the book is the years of preparation behind it. Yet all the research and reflection might have produced a factually correct but flat work were the author not a genuine novelist who carries his learning lightly, knows how to tell a tragic story, and makes us care about his characters.

At first glance the central character Graham Lamb, sheriff of Winnemucca, fits the conventions of the western. Stoic, laconic, tough, he has killed a man and knows how to apply the third degree to get a confession. A closer look reveals a multifaceted person—shrewd,

---

2   David Rio, "Basques in the International West: An Interview with Frank Bergon," *Western American Literature*, 36 (Spring 2001), 64-65. Battle Mountain is 35 miles from the site of the massacre. The novel includes maps of key Nevada locales on the inside front and back covers.

3   Frank Bergon, "The Search for Shoshone Mike," *Nevada Magazine* (November-December 1987): 57-59.

4   Frank Bergon, "How to Know What to Write," talk at Center of the American West, Boulder, CO., April 29, 2016.

contemplative, tolerant, sensitive. Lamb's relationship with his wife Nellie is striking. Several chapters show how acutely observant he is of her, how their give-and-take talks capture both the strains in and strengths of their love. Nellie is also complex. She admires the civilization of San Francisco, terms the Indians "savages," yet welcomes the chance to come home and kill her own chickens. Known for his unflappable calm and "wait and see" attitude, Lamb serves as a mediator between contending groups; he sees his job as enabling "different people to live in different ways without killing each other."[5] A student of fallible human nature, he wants the law to be firm but flexible, making allowances for various codes, cultures, and prejudices. Thus he keeps the solid daytime citizens separate from their less respectable nocturnal counterparts.

Shoshone Mike is both a western and a murder mystery. When the novel opens in 1911, four men, three of them Basque sheepherders, have been found dead in Little High Rock Canyon and a posse is searching for the killers. Sheriff Lamb is known for always getting his man; he "solves" crimes not scouring the countryside but waiting for reliable facts and valid reasons to emerge before making his move. Yet in this case, he is at first mistaken. He thinks the perpetrators were "some riffraff and thieves" like Frank Tranmer and Nimrod Urie. It takes time before he puts the pieces together and understands what led up to the four murders and who was responsible. In the novel's second section, set in the previous year, we learn that a man named Frankie Dopp had been killed, supposedly by some Indians he caught changing brands on stolen horses, and Lamb suspects Tranmer and Urie. What he doesn't know yet is that the person those two desperados *had* killed was Shoshone Mike's son Jack, and that Mike's band killed Dopp to avenge that previous murder. Under questioning, Urie insists that Shoshones killed Dopp, but Lamb thinks he's lying. Only after the four men are found dead in the canyon, and more information is discovered, does Lamb admit that he had been wrong, that the posse was now in hot pursuit of "a Shoshone family"(212).

The novel's thirty-five chapters juxtapose the points of view of key characters; among the most impressive are those devoted to Shoshone Mike and his daughter Henie. Bergon's short, declarative sentences, marked by telling details that evoke a sense of place and the spirit of a people, capture the essentials of a besieged culture. Since the Shoshone have been confined to reservations for forty years, Mike is a walking anachronism;

---

5   Frank Bergon, *Shoshone Mike* (New York: Viking, 1987), 11. Subsequent quotes cited parenthetically.

he fashions ropes, arrows, spears, and headdresses in traditional ways, knows how to move with the seasons, live off the land, and attend to the power of dreams. The author's clear, crisp style shows us the world as the Shoshone experienced it, painting the Nevada landscape so vividly as the seasons change that it, too, becomes a major character:

> The winds grew warmer. The ice broke up in the creek. Trout swam in the creek and squirrels pushed themselves out of the ground. Their noses quivered as they looked at the world with quick dark eyes. Green clover appeared along the stream. Shoots of wild onions and the light green leaves of young lettuce thickened on the canyon floor. After the winter, they tasted like sunlight and spring water. Birds were flying around everywhere. (77)

Mike's Wolf and Coyote tales teach his children about the animistic forces of nature and how the Shoshone, known to themselves as "the People," fit into the grand scheme of things. Henie keenly notes that the abandoned nests of sparrows are lined with the same shredded sagebrush bark as the floor of her wickiup. She appreciates that her world, before the disruption of whites, was "a satisfactory place to live"(77). After one of his sons kills Dopp, however, Mike and his family must "live like the blue summer haze and the winter fog"(75), struggling to survive in the seams between the encroaching whites and the degradations of reservation life. Like his contemporary Ishi, the last "wild" Indian in California, Mike faces extinction. He and his family strive to maintain an ancient way of life that is perishing from a thousand cuts. "We're vanishing," he tells Henie. "I don't know why this is happening. I don't think we are useless"(224).

The second section of the novel ends with Henie's brief account of how four men, who weren't tracking Mike's band, see a few butchered cattle in the snow and walk into a lethal ambush. The third section, "Battle at Rabbit Creek," relates the tragic consequence of these murders. The point of view now shifts for a time to Mort West, a young member of the posse determined "to prove he was as game"(160) as the other men. For him the expedition, in spite of the posse's petty feuds and one-upmanship struggles, is a rite of passage into manhood. On the other hand, Jean Erramouspe, a "black Basco," is not allowed to join them and avenge his father, one of the four murdered men. This highly prejudiced posse is only seeking to inflict justice for the single "white man" killed.

The leader of the posse, Captain J. P. Donnelley, deliberately misleads Lamb about how close they are to Mike's band. As a result, Lamb is not present for the battle at Rabbit Creek. Instead, the fighting is rendered through the point of view of Mort West. First he sees a young girl running, screaming a warning, then four armed warriors coming forward from the camp. Amid the ensuing gunfire someone shouts, "Shoot the horses," and Mort sees:

> the girl up and running again toward the camp as the last of the horses threw its head toward the sky and slumped to the ground. . . . There was a volley of shots and the black head dropped behind sagebrush. "I got him this time," someone shouted. The head popped up again and a rifle cracked. A running form collapsed into the brush. The men fired at the spot where the form disappeared, only to be answered by a shot several yards to the left of where they were shooting. (236-237)

Here the impressionistic prose captures the frantic you-are-there immediacy of battle, how it feels to be in the midst of a life-and-death fight where confusion reigns and what is seen one second is refuted by what happens next. Isolated images jump out for a second, creating a somewhat surreal effect: "the toe of Skinny's boot showing over the cantle as he hung from the side of his horse"(237); a teenage girl charging with a spear; "a black spot" suddenly appearing on the forehead of an Indian woman, killing her instantly. Mort experiences the daze, the bafflement of the bloody engagement that leaves four Indian men, two women, and two young boys, as well as one of the posse, dead. All he can think at the end is, "He had expected something different"(250); while Lamb, upon his belated arrival at a battle he had hoped to prevent, can only cry out, "What in hell has been going on here?"(249).

By having Lamb arrive too late to stop the killing, if that were possible, Bergon keeps faith with the historical record. Although back in Winnemucca the members of the posse are celebrated as heroes, in truth there were none. For his part Lamb is filled with despair that the tragedy wasn't averted. He engages in three important conversations in the final chapters about the meaning of what happened and whether the massacre was inevitable. One is with Father Enright, a voice of Christian witness, who had previously delivered a sermon about treating people, especially enemies, like the good Samaritan and leaving vengeance to the Lord:

> "We talk about bringing the kingdom of heaven into this world," the priest said, "but it's not possible. The violent bear it away."
>
> "Bear what away?" Lamb asked. . . . "You have to remember that those Indians murdered innocent people. They had wives, families, friends"
>
> "We did to them exactly what we said they were going to do to us. What does that make us?"(269)

Lamb understands why the posse didn't spare most of Mike's family, but that doesn't mean he condones the killing. His wife Nellie, on the other hand, has no remorse. For her the Indians "were out of the dark ages. Those boys had a job to do and they did it," while Lamb wanted them treated no differently than those white killers, Tranmer and Urie: "Why couldn't they be caught and tried just like anybody else?"(278). As sheriff, he thinks the laws should apply equally to all, but it is an open question whether for Mike it was more "just" to die in battle or at the end of a rope, a form of death all Indians loathed.

The crucial question was whether the tragedy was inevitable. It has been a standard and self-serving interpretation of the Indian wars since their inception that the beliefs and customs of Native Americans were doomed, that they were backward peoples who must of necessity yield to civilization and progress. Lamb doesn't see it that way. In a last discussion with Donnelley, he admits that the boys in the posse "were brave. . . . They really didn't know what they were up against, and they stuck it out"(281), but he doesn't approve of the wanton killing that took place. Even if Mike's band insisted on fighting, some deaths might have been prevented. "If we hadn't wiped them out," Donnelley states, "somebody else would've. It was inevitable." To which Lamb replies, "Nothing's inevitable . . . especially that"(282). Indeed, as the novel makes clear, there were contingencies throughout the story. Had the four men, for example, not happened upon slaughtered steers in the snow, they would not have been killed, there would have been no posse, Shoshone Mike's family might have hidden in the wilderness areas of Nevada and Idaho and survived for years.

And yet, as the Afterword reminds us, we are all born to die. Ishi lived out his last days at the University of California Museum of Anthropology; within eighteen months of the battle, Henie and two more of Mike's children, like many confined to reservations, died of disease. Only the baby "recovered and grew up as Mary Josephine Estep"(288). Many years later she was interviewed by the author of this memorable novel, already an acknowledged classic.

The Temptations of St. Ed & Brother S

Frank was educated in Jesuit schools, and a sabbatical year trip to Spain in 1984 rekindled his interest in monks and mysticism. He visited monasteries and read *The Cloud of Unknowing* and other essential works about devotional practices that date to the desert fathers.[6] It is this age-old tradition that the novel's protagonists, St. Ed and Brother S, hope to revive. Known to be a little "wacky," St. Ed is an erudite student of monasticism and, following in the footsteps of his fellow Basque Ignatius of Loyola, he wants to found a transformative religious order. His star recruit, Brother S, aspires "to be a saint."[7] Back in high school, "as he listened to pop songs on the radio, he yearned for that transcendent experience the mystics described as ecstasy"(5). The question is whether Brother S has a true vocation, or is just a California guy auditioning a unique lifestyle. Their crucial concern is a nuclear waste site at Shoshone Mountain[8] that threatens their makeshift monastery as well as the future of the planet. St. Ed wants to harness spiritual energy so that "the Cloud of Unknowing [will]. . . overwhelm faith in the mushroom cloud"(24). But temptation promptly arrives in the form of Amy Chávez, rescued from the desert by Brother S. During her recovery he sees her sunbathing naked on a log; afterwards she cuts her finger, which he "thrust . . . into his mouth"(121) to stop the bleeding. From then on, two plot lines compete: can the nuclear waste site be stopped? And will Amy's presence break the vows of St. Ed and Brother S?

---

6   Rio, Bergon Interview, 66. My wife Roser and I accompanied Frank and Holly St. John Bergon on excursions in Catalonia to see the splendid monasteries of Santes Creus and Poblet, the latter still vibrantly active.

7   Frank Bergon, *The Temptations of St. Ed & Brother S* (Reno: University of Nevada Press, 1993), 9. Subsequent quotes cited parenthetically.

8   The actual site was Yucca Mountain. While remaining true to the basic historical situation regarding nuclear waste disposal, the novel changes other names and places and creates the principal characters and plot.

Thomas Merton, who knew whereof he spoke, provides a key to why the mission of St. Ed and Brother S will be marked by folly and probably doomed to failure: "The most dangerous person in the world is an unfulfilled mystic"(77). Striving to rise above the quotidian and achieve perfection can result in unforeseen and sometimes disastrous consequences. One of the novel's strengths is St. Ed's ability to find analogies for their monastic efforts in anecdotes about the desert fathers and the founders of religious orders; these serve as reminders, even as a typology, highlighting the recurrent patterns inherent in the contemplative life. The fundamental irony, however, which provides a wealth of comic insights as well as a few tragic outcomes, is that knowing the accomplishments as well as the mistakes of the past does not mean that one can achieve the former and prevent the latter in the present.

Historically, sexual temptations have presented a crucial challenge to monastic life as well as priestly chastity. Often the temptations faced by the desert fathers were erotic. Fasting and abstinence may induce visions, but they can also stimulate desire. If sex is not accepted as a natural part of life, it becomes, to the tormented mind, unnatural, demonic. Thus there is an unfortunate connection between mysticism and misogyny. While St. Francis and St. Dominic "made room for women in their reform of monasticism"(124), others in the Church denounced the carnality of females as evil. Amy exudes "a good-natured innocence," but Brother S notes she has "bedroom eyes"(73). Before long, her role in the monks' desert retreat becomes that of Eve in the garden.

When Amy's brutal boyfriend Jerry badly beats Brother S, to soothe him she "took off her clothes and spread her body over his like a comforting angel"(130). Although they then live "separately and chastely"(148), Brother S is smitten and tells St. Ed, "I feel we've lost our way"(155). St. Ed also falls for Amy's allure, even after, or perhaps especially because, she announces, "I want to be a monk"(161). Simultaneously we have the on-going saga of her stolen pink panties, fetishized by both men, who reify her into a temptress, "a demon of fornication"(207). Thus we see how these two would-be holy men put the blame on Amy for their own twisted lust.

St. Ed makes a convincing case for the lethal dangers posed by nuclear waste. He knows the site was chosen because Nevada is a thinly populated state whose vast spaces lend themselves to exploitation. Furthermore, the feds have selected a mountain sacred to the Shoshone. St. Ed provides authentic information about the monastic tradition and eloquently argues for the concepts of sacramental time and eternal life as well. Yet his determination to start a monastic renaissance and stop construction at the nuclear waste site are all too easily sidetracked by his propensity to outsmart himself. When he takes a pair of Amy's panties supposedly to get her to confess another pair had been stolen, we suspect ulterior motives. He diagnoses her as a "gymnomaniac,"[9] a person who shuns clothes, only to "convert" her into keeping them on. Then he proclaims her "Mother Amy," abbess of the monastery, and primes his postulants for "spiritual delight in eternal time"(224). Shortly after, Amy, who seems quite sincere in her new vocation, is shot by a paranoid hermit named Straightgut, and the resulting chaos shatters St. Ed's schemes.

No one is more unhinged by Amy's near-fatal injury than Brother S, who even before that bizarre event suffered a sudden paralysis of one arm that he saw as just punishment for ever touching her. This psychosomatic illness seems to free him, for a time, from "all his sharp longing for Amy"(174). In his quest for a cure, he even attends a precisely observed peyote ceremony.

When finally he regains use of his arm, he feels he has been redeemed, but the truth is he was never in love with Amy but rather self-absorbed in his own desires.[10] He accuses St. Ed of being "evil. . . . I know the devil has your heart"(225-26) for favoring Amy, and during her hospitalization he slips into a downward spiral where he attends a burlesque show and then does a brief stint as a disc jockey, playing pop love songs from his adolescence and feeling sorry for himself. Because he no longer visits Amy, he is unaware of her miraculous recovery, and, in a vain attempt to protect Straightgut, granted refuge by St. Ed, from the murderous intentions of Jerry, Brother S destroys himself, driving off in a tractor on a Quixotic suicidal strike against the nuclear waste facility at Shoshone Mountain. In his final delusion, rendered in heightened poetic prose, he believes he has pierced the encroaching darkness and attained the ecstasy he has always sought—"Eternal light"(294).

---

9   A gymnosophist was "a member of an ancient Hindu sect of ascetics who wore little or no clothing." *Webster's New World Dictionary* (New York: Simon & Schuster, 1980), 625.

10   Brother S is disturbed by his "engorged, aching" penis (152). "Even St. Augustine found erections so beyond human control that he was convinced they were proof of man's lack of free will" (152). This is true: when he was sixteen Augustine was shamed by unwanted erections at the public baths, which made him wonder why he couldn't prevent them by sheer will power. He eventually concluded that we are born innately evil. Thus his theology contains the dogmas of original sin and infant damnation, two notions that did more harm than good and which tie into the novel's exploration of what is natural and unnatural in human sexuality.

Not surprisingly, St. Ed has earned the ire of his bishop, who warns him "we're not some disembodied spirits who can put off our bodies and take hot baths with girls and remain sexually pure.... Christianity keeps us in the real world, in the flesh as we are, not in some crazy never-never land where people can somehow float out of their bodies into some spiritual cloud"(266-267). Wise words, but St. Ed isn't about to give up his grand design. He sees himself as a martyr who had "been calumniated, abused, jailed, and suppressed for his efforts to bring spiritual reforms to the slack soul of the nuclear age"(300), and Amy is determined not to permit Brother S's "life and death [to] be meaningless"(303). In the end a motley crew of seven believers set out to "choose the Cloud of Unknowing—in this world"(305). Will they succeed? Not likely, given the novel's tragi-comic vision of human nature. But that's not to say their spiritual venture isn't worth another try.

Wild Game

Wild Game dramatizes a clash of values between Old West ideals and New West realities. The novel draws upon the true story of Claude Dallas, who killed two game wardens seeking to arrest him for poaching in his remote Idaho camp. Since he lived as a self-reliant Mountain Man, eluded a posse, convinced a jury he acted in his own defense, then escaped from prison and avoided recapture for a time, the media made him a mythic hero while vilifying his victims. Featured in the news, he was the subject of a TV film and two non-fiction books.[11] He seemed to be a reincarnation of the admired "outlaw" figures of the frontier who shoot to kill and abide by their own rules. Like Shoshone Mike, Claude Dallas was an anachronism, a person who consciously modeled himself after the fantasy cowboys in Louis L'Amour novels and Marlboro Man ads. His fame in the 1980s coincided with the Sagebrush Rebellion in the West, a populist movement supported by President Reagan. At issue was "an intensifying conflict between an environmentalist, recreational West and a diminishing

---

11 Jeff Long, *Outlaw: The True Story of Claude Dallas* (New York: William Morrow, 1985); Jack Olson, *Give a Boy a Gun: A True Story of Law and Disorder in the American West* (New York: Delacorte Press, 1985). While both books contain factual material of interest about the murders and the trial, each author lacks a moral compass when it comes to Dallas, accepting his highly suspect version of events, indulging in pure apologetics for his lethal actions, and drawing inadequate conclusions about the meaning of his "true story."

mining, grazing, and logging West."[12] Thus Claude Dallas, in spite of the innocent blood on his hands, was celebrated as an ultimate individualist who stood up to federal authority.

For Bergon, Claude Dallas was an "ersatz survivalist," while the real heroes were the two murdered men who had devoted their lives to protecting "wild game."[13] The challenge was to create a novel where Billy Crockett (roughly based on Dallas), and the issues he embodies can be seen in a more complex way and historical facts are combined with emotional and moral truths. The main character Jack Irigaray, a Basque wildlife biologist, accompanies his friend Bob Pritchard and another Nevada warden Larry Hughes when they try to arrest Crockett in Little High Rock Canyon for "trash trapping" and killing game out of season. The setting is early January, 1982, and the men find ample evidence of Crockett's illegal activities, to which he boldly admits: "I'm a hundred miles from civilization. If I obeyed city people's laws, I'd starve to death. . . . It's a matter of survival."[14]

What happens next is sudden and brutal. As Jack is looking inside Crockett's tent, he hears Pritchard cry out, "Oh, no!" and then shots. Whirling around, Jack sees Crockett in a crouching position fire a handgun at Bob and Larry, retrieve a .22 rifle from the tent, and shoot both men in the head. In terror for his own life, Jack helps Crockett cover up the crime. A half-naked Hughes is dumped in an ice-laden creek and Pritchard's body is last seen in the back of a pickup. At the conclusion of this harrowing first chapter, presented from Jack's point of view, Crockett smirks, says "Sorry, Jack," and shoots him too.

Found the next morning, Jack survives; he wonders if Crockett, a crack shot, meant to kill him. He is tormented by regrets that he didn't do more to prevent the deaths and by an obsessive notion that he and Crockett were in a deadly "wild game" of their own. To "redeem himself" (53), Jack wants to capture the killer and find Bob's body, while his wife Beth pleads with him to save their rocky marriage and "Put this thing behind you" (63). For Jack, figuring out how Crockett thinks is the key to capturing him. In a memorable chapter, Jack interviews his Uncle Pete, who once employed

---

12 Frank Bergon, "Rebellion in Marlboro Country," *Two-Buck Chuck & The Marlboro Man: The New Old West.* (Reno: University of Nevada Press, 2019), 200. Dallas once worked for the brother of Frank's uncle and godfather. "The true story of the West," Bergon notes, "is not independence but interdependence."
13 Rio, Bergon Interview, 65.
14 Frank Bergon, *Wild Game* (Reno: University of Nevada Press, 1995), 21. Subsequent quotes cited parenthetically.

Billy on his ranch. A sharply drawn character, Pete epitomizes the best values of the Old West. He taught Crockett the skills to be a true cowboy, a buckaroo. "Nothing came easy to Billy," Pete says, "but he worked hard at learning"(87), and for Pete hard work ranks with "good judgment and physical competence as signs of virtue"(90). While he doesn't approve of Billy's law-breaking, Pete admires how "he just wanted to do things the way the old timers did"(95). In effect, Billy writes his own script, plays the part, and becomes the character he pretends to be.

Jack as a boy also worked for Pete and has always admired him. Beth suggests that he may admire Billy as well: "He acted out what you dreamed about"(104). Perhaps because Billy is his "secret sharer," Jack decides that "the desire to kill Crockett and the demon inside him were one and the same"(122). Yet in the final pursuit that leads to his surrender, it is Billy who shoots at Jack twice: "I could've killed you, Basco. That makes three times. Don't forget"(142). Jack replies that it's time to "end this game"(151) and for Crockett to tell where Bob's body is, but he is keeping his own counsel in anticipation of his trial.

"It's going to come down to his word against yours"(154), Jack is warned by his friend Jim Sandoval about what to expect in court. The four chapters on the trial are a *Rashomon*-like tour de force, pitting Jack's honest attempt to relate what he witnessed against Billy's ability to twist the truth in his favor. A lawyer once told me that the secret to winning a case was to present the jury with a convincing "cartoon," an oversimplified version of events slanted to favor a client. Jack conscientiously tries to tell what happened, but because he was in the tent during the exchange that led up to the shooting and was repeatedly asked to recall exactly what he saw and heard, the defense exploits slight inconsistencies in his account.[15] As a result, a local paper states that Jack's "whole testimony was perceived as convoluted and contradictory"(167). Billy, on the other hand, has his story down pat. "Composed, confident, idealistic, he blossomed into a man from another era"(174). He looks so much like the authentic cowboys he imitates that an AP reporter proclaims him, "The Real Thing"(174).

Billy's self-serving version was that an overbearing Pritchard was "flying hot" at him from the start, frequently reaching for his gun and threatening, "You can go easy or you can go hard, Crockett"(177), which is to say dead

---

15   While the murders themselves and the proceedings of the trial are similar to the Claude Dallas case, Jack is a completely different character than Jim Stevens, the potato farmer who witnessed the shooting. The creation of Jack enables Bergon to provide richer dramatic texture and deeper moral meanings to the story.

or alive. Billy argued that this was his home and he needed to kill wild game to survive, and Bob replied, " 'I can carry you out. . . .' Then he went for his gun. . . .He fired one round at me. Then I fired"(178–179), hitting both Pritchard and Hughes. As to why he proceeded to shoot them in the head, Billy said "I was a little crazy at that stage. . . . I was afraid for my life"(179). He didn't kill Jack because he was unarmed, and he denied Jack's sworn statement that he fired from a combat crouch and later confessed, "This is murder one for me"(181). When he did shoot Jack it was because he "came at me with a shovel"(180). The defense is permitted to slander Bob as a bully and reveal that Jack is an alcoholic, yet the judge doesn't allow testimony that Billy possessed an arsenal of assault weapons and read books on combat firefights. Although the prosecution noted that "by his own admission"(195) Crockett had broken the law, resisted arrest, and killed two men who were doing their duty, the Nevada jury, swayed by myths of the Old West, believed Billy's improbable story and only found him guilty of voluntary manslaughter. "We just figured Pritchard drew his gun and Crockett was a better marksman," the foreman said—but for those "excessive" shots to the head, Billy would have gotten off scot free(205).

On an apt ironic note, at the sentencing hearing the apparently lenient judge cuts through the fog of obfuscation and bluntly states, "I don't believe the issue of self-defense ever arose at Little High Rock Canyon"(211). To decide otherwise, as the jury has, "is an insult to common sense"(212). He then proceeds to outline the most likely scenario and sentences Billy to the maximum penalty of thirty years. After months of torment, Jack feels vindicated: "the judge had believed him, not Crockett"(217). Yet his troubles are not over, since the entire experience has left him disoriented and in despair. His deteriorating marriage to Beth ends in an uncontested divorce. Even before Billy reveals where Bob is buried, Jack gets involved with his grieving widow Cindy. Then, to make matters worse, he has an affair with Billy's former girlfriend Georgette and visits a prostitute. He believes that "women control the game of love"(199), proceeds to look for love in all the wrong places, and succumbs to a self-inflicted moral and mental collapse. Instead of seeing Georgette as highly suspect for having been with Billy in the first place, Jack harbors macho fears that Billy is better with women and more of a man than he is. At the end of his untenable relationship with Georgette, she shouts, "You're not like Billy at all. You're a fucking animal"(258). In sum, Jack makes a series of bad decisions without understanding why he is losing his self-respect and dignity. He remains trapped in some "wild game" with Billy Crockett.

When Billy escapes four years later, Jack is on "the rebound from booze," having lost "his wife, his girlfriend, his car, his license, his job" (272). At a final confrontation, Jack tracks Billy down in Mexico, where Billy boasts about outwitting the jury and being his own man: "Nobody lived out in the country the way I did. . . . It was people like you who ruined it" (294). Jack, at last, sees through Billy's bravado: "You're not tough, Billy. You're mean, but you're not tough" (295). After Billy is recaptured, he once again bamboozles a jury by pleading, in effect, paranoia: he only fled for fear of his life. Nonetheless, he will still have to serve many years before the prospect of parole. For his part, Jack finally develops the good judgment to come to terms with who he is. And he understands that the most common pattern of the natural world is not survival of the fittest but peaceful coexistence. At the novel's end, he is a warden protecting the wild game he loves.

Jesse's Ghost

The novel's opening tells us that this is "The story of how I came to kill my best friend," and its Bob Dylan epigraph concludes "Go get my pistol, babe, / I can't tell right from wrong."[16] As in Gabriel García Márquez's masterpiece *Chronicle of a Death Foretold*, a murder is announced at the start and the narrative explores what led up to it. *Jesse's Ghost* was inspired by a crime that involved several of Bergon's boyhood friends from his hometown of Madera, California. In Fresno on September 4, 1968, Gary Bolding shot Orville Lee Carter, known as Billy, for sleeping with his estranged wife Coann Swift Garvey.[17] Unlike the sensationalized Claude Dallas case, this was the kind of killing that never draws national attention, precisely because it was ordinary. The challenge for the author, then, is to bring the characters alive so that we understand who they are and care about this particular domestic tragedy. Since Frank knew the participants and was involved in key events, much of his research consisted of interviews. Jesse Floyd is based on Billy Carter, while Sonny Childers, the narrator, is a composite drawn from multiple sources. This is also true of his wife Sonia and other characters. Likewise Mitch and Ana Etcheverry and their

---

16 Frank Bergon, *Jesse's Ghost* (Berkeley, CA: Heyday, 2011), 1. Subsequent quotes cited parenthetically.
17 Bill Coate, "Pieces of the Past," *Madera Tribune* (June 1, 2011), 2. This article includes the original account of the crime in *The Fresno Bee* (September 4, 1968).

parents share similarities with the Bergon family, but in the novel they are created figures with their own motivations.

An essential essay, "The Toughest Kid We Knew," recounts the recollections of Frank and his friends. They all agreed that Billy Carter was the toughest fighter in the San Joaquin Valley and possessed immense personal charm. "Billy was an all-American Boy," one said. "He had crystal-clear blue eyes, a great smile, he was a hard worker, and a loyal friend."[18] Others praised his smarts, wit, and gift for gab. They were all in awe of his prowess as a no-holds-barred brawler and envied his success with the opposite sex. At a time when Frank felt "tongue-tied and fearful of being trapped by wily women," Billy was a smooth talker, "a magnet for girls" in part because he possessed "the power of the outlaw." Even though as a "pure Okie"[19] he lacked status, Billy dated the daughters of a dentist, a doctor, and a businessman. This would suggest that Madera was free of snobbery, yet social undercurrents prevented him from marrying the girl of his choice and the resultant mismatches, leaving several women in love with him, led to his violent death.

When the novel begins Sonny has served his time in prison and, thanks to Father Dan's teachings, thinks he's reformed and happy with his new wife: "People say there are two kinds of women: those you love and those you marry. But that's not true for me. I love Lynette and I loved Sonia"(3). But it's an open question whether Sonny really has changed his life or knows what love is. The arrival of his old friend Mitch, who is haunted by Jesse's murder and wants to understand it, probes old wounds and leads Sonny to confess, "I don't know what got into me"(32). At the time, he was at the mercy of unconscious forces, and as he relates his life we realize that he still hasn't come to terms with who he is and how the values of the valley have shaped him. Both Jessie and Sonny were "Okie riffraff"(4), products of an ages old Scots-Irish clan culture that stressed fierce individualism, fundamental equality, defiance of authority, and a man's pride in defending his honor with his fists or other weapons. It was these feisty and relentless frontiersmen who were the bane of American Indians from the Appalachians to the Far West, and who fought with great valor in our foreign wars.[20] "Jesse just loved to fight," and Sonny shares

---

18 Frank Bergon, "The Toughest Kid We Knew," in *The Toughest Kid We Knew: The Old New West: A Personal History* (Reno: University of Nevada Press, 2020), 178. Mitch says these words in the novel, p. 24.

19 Bergon, "Toughest Kid," 182, 179, 180, 181.

20 See Arthur Herman, *How the Scots Invented the Modern World* (New York: Crown Publishing, 2001), and James Webb, *Born Fighting: How the Scots-Irish Shaped America* (New York: Broadway Books, 2004).

his enthusiasm: "There's no better feeling than kicking the shit out of somebody"(35), an assumption that often ruled their young lives. While he rarely seeks out his battles, Jesse never backs down from a challenge, and his reputation for toughness, just like the man known to be the fastest gun, draws many an upstart to test his mettle against him.

While *Jesse's Ghost* is packed with blow-by-blow accounts of the fights Jesse and Sonny were in—mostly victories but a few bloody defeats—their relationships with women are what proves to be lethal. Near the end of Part I, Lynette suddenly announces, "I'm leaving you, Sonny" and adds that she considers their seventeen years together "a mistake"(37). That he didn't see trouble brewing is a sign of Sonny's ineptitude with women, yet it leads him to speculate about previous romantic entanglements at the core of the plot: "No one forgets their first love. Ana loved me, and I loved her. Sonia loved Jessie but married me. Ana loved Jesse, but he loved Sonia. We were all hooked up in a crisscrossed love that never got straight." He then admits that he probably hated Jesse, and may have shot him, "because I loved him"(39).

Part II goes back in time to re-create the summer it all began: Jesse and Sonny were best friends, fresh out of high school, tending tomatoes for Mitch's father Sam. After a day of hard work, "at night we tomcatted around until morning"(43). Sonny's first love is Ana, Mitch's fourteen-year-old sister. When he informs Sam he wants to marry his daughter, he shrewdly keeps cool and tells Sonny he's a good worker but simply "can't afford it"(52). Later he advises Sonny to stop partying and settle down before someone gets hurt. One reason they want to run off is that their mothers are alcoholics: Ana's, in particular, made her home "a screaming hell"(45). In truth, life in the valley is very hard on all the women, many of whom "are going crazy with booze"(52) and grow old before their time. It's a macho culture, and Sonny's idea of courtship is shooting rabbits or rats or gigging for frogs. Jesse is more sophisticated with women; he asks, "Why don't you take Ana out on a proper date?"(50). Jesse, for his part, plays the field. Sonny knows that he "was never going to attract girls the way he did"(121). Jesse chooses Sonia for the summer, detailing their sexual exploits to Sonny, but when they break up, she targets Sonny, telling him "You're my sweetheart" and assuring him "I am not pregnant"(138). Shortly afterwards, Sonny sees Jesse "putting the wood to Ana"(140). Sonny learns that Sonia's father had forbidden her to "marry that Okie kid"(155); as a result Jesse has turned to Ana. In spite of this tangled web, with Sonny wondering whether Sonia was using him to make Jesse jealous, the pair marries: "We were happy, Sonia and me, for a while, in our way"(159). Jesse then marries Ana, and the couples go off in different directions—for a time.

Sonny's narrative voice is compelling; like Huck Finn, another Scots-Irish boy who tells his own story, Sonny is acculturated to his valley. As it never occurs to Huck that slavery is wrong (he's going to hell for being a rotten kid and helping his friend Jim), so Sonny rarely questions a life centered on working, drinking, fighting, and fucking. He takes these things for granted just as Buck Grangerford accepts feuding.[21] Like Huck's "Pap," Sonny's father was "a real mean person"(70), while his stepfather Dewey, a brawler and heavy drinker, "whopped"(82) him to teach him manners. To his credit, Dewey "learned"(65) Sonny the right way to work. Indeed, some of the strongest passages in the novel are on farm work in the valley. As a boy Sonny cut grapes, dug potatoes, rolled trays, chopped and picked cotton, but Sam's "Tomato Piece" is described the most memorably. Sonny and Jesse were responsible for irrigating the fields, and in those days, when planes dropped carcinogenic bug spray on workers, no one cared. Like Huck on the Mississippi, Sonny's descriptions of the natural world can be poetic: "Outside, when I looked across the sparkling alfalfa at the sun coming up above the Sierras I felt in a new country. A breeze smelled of eucalyptus leaves and Mrs. Etcheverry's flowers. Even the blazing sun bounced as it popped up fresh from the Nevada desert behind the mountains. The whole ranch shined full of light, something familiar but strange"(105); "Moonlight brightened the ditch water creeping over the ground like slow-moving mercury as it twisted around the alfalfa stalks, giving the air a sweet, musty smell. You could almost hear the water crackle through the hay stubble"(125). Sonny's narrative, at its best, is simple, sensuous, direct, lyrical, with the right admixture of slang and common, and sometimes uncommon, usage. To select one example: "If he wanted to plug Ana, I thought, and she was abiding, well, then, more power to him"(146). The surprise choice is "abiding," but it is spot on to Sonny's particular world. Finally, like Huck asking Jim if the stars were made or just happened, occasionally Sonny ponders ultimate questions: "I wondered which would be better, being a ghost and knowing yourself dead or just being dead without knowing it"(130).

---

21   "Well," says Buck, "a feud is this way. A man has a quarrel with another man, and kills him, and then that other man's brother kills *him*, then the other brothers, on both sides, goes for one another, then the *cousins* chip in—and by and by everybody's killed off, and there ain't no more feud. But it's kind of slow, and takes a long time." Mark Twain, *The Adventures of Huckleberry Finn* (Berkeley: University of California Press, 1985), 146.

A few years pass. Mitch comes home from college to find his mother dead in her bedroom from alcoholism; Sam moves to town and starts drinking too. After multiple amputations, Dewey dies of diabetes. Jesse and Sonny join the National Guard: "We started having good times again . . . but always without our wives"(169). Jesse now heads his family septic business; he is "a honey pumper" who lives with Ana in "a rundown white-board house"(172) with their young son. Sonny and Sonia have a girl, but "things slid south between us. She was bound to look down on me when she saw the situation she found herself in"(174–175). Clearly, both Ana and Sonia are dissatisfied that their husbands have not risen on the social ladder, and, as happens in many failing marriages, red lines are crossed and unsayable words spoken. Sonia calls Sonny "a fucking wino loser"(174), a coward, and challenges him to "Go fuck Jesse. That's what you wanted with me anyway"(177). Sonny resists an urge to hit her and goes off on another drunk. Soon afterwards, the couple separates, Jesse resumes sleeping with Sonia, a pregnant Ana is in despair, and Sonny is at the end of his tether. Since their divorce is not finalized, Sonny thinks he can get Sonia back. "You two aren't stomping on me no more," he declares. "He's not going to have you," to which Sonia replies, "Have me? . . . He can have me whenever he wants"(184).

Criminal psychologists have long pointed out that uttering certain unsayable things that touch upon repressed feelings can trigger an uncontrollable violent response. Some variation of this is what happens in Sonny's case. After he traces the couple to a motel, he buys a .38 pistol and begins to stalk his estranged wife. Fuel is added to the fire when Jesse says in a phone conversation, "She's left you. . . . Forget it, Sonny. You know you were always second choice"(184–185). The next time Sonny sees Jesse he kills him, firing two shots at Sonia as well. At the trial, because his lawyer portrays Jesse as "violent, aggressive, and dangerous," Sonny is merely convicted of voluntary manslaughter, yet he knows in his heart that he "had murdered Jesse"(189), and like Mitch he is still haunted by Jesse's ghost.

Mitch is researching an article prior to writing a book on the murder; he is the one who gets Sonny to relate what led up to the killing and thus it falls on his shoulders to make sense of events. Since he's been to college and lived away from the valley for years, we expect him to have a larger perspective. During the summer when the three friends worked at irrigating Sam's tomatoes, Mitch told Sonny, "Someday we're probably going to look back on this as the best time of our life"(76). Sonny doesn't know how to respond: "Here we were without pussy, busted up from hangovers, smeared with mud and goose shit, threatened by three thugs," if that was the best of times, "I hated to think what would be the worst"(76–77). In this instance, Sonny is wiser than Mitch, who wants to celebrate those glory days, regardless of the cost in life and limb. Indeed, when worse times come, Mitch's interpretation of the tragedy is muted. He tells Sonny, in relation to Jesse's death, "Live by the sword, die by the sword"(195), since Jesse "brought it on himself"(196), and that he had forgiven Sonny and had no hard feelings. He brings unwelcome news that "Sonia still carries a torch for Jesse" and that "Ana's bitter about everything . . . except Jesse" (194). On a more positive note, Mitch tells Sonny he has talked to Lynette and a reconciliation is possible. Father Dan, for his part, is trying to teach Sonny "the difference between loving and fucking"(191). That Sonny finds comfort in religion fits another aspect of valley culture. Although he hopes to make a new start, at the end he is a figure of pathos: "I always knew I was second pickings"(199), an all-too apt metaphor for a man who worked the tomato fields of the San Joaquin Valley.

One final irony eludes Mitch and Sonny. While both admired Jesse as the Alpha Male of their world, what was he actually thinking? What did he aspire to be? Obviously he used his fists to rise to the top of his immediate physical world. But what about his social world? He was a poor Okie boy who married an attractive girl from a land-owning family, sported a fancy car, and hoped to make enough money to buy a big house, yet as a "honey pumper" he was trapped in a lower status. Thus he burned "the candle at both ends"(180) to compensate. In a sense, Mitch is right, Jesse *did* bring destruction down on his own head. Yet if Mitch wanted to be Jesse, in his heart of hearts Jesse's dream was to be Mitch.

Frank Bergon's four novels deserve attention largely due to description, dialogue, and drama. Each presents a vividly evoked shared landscape that encompasses Nevada and the San Joaquin Valley. A sense of place shapes the participants in the stories. Where you are is a part of who you are. The central characters, sharply individualized and fully realized, not only talk to each other, they talk *back*, giving voice to various points of view. The resulting clash of values creates the essential conflict. Each novel features an anachronistic and controversial way of life—Shoshone Mike's roving band of renegades. St. Ed's efforts to revive an ancient monastic tradition, Billy Crockett's determination to survive as a mountain man beyond the law, and Jesse Floyd's sustained prowess as a fighter and womanizer. Each of these challenges meets strong opposition and ends in defeat or death. Yet each dramatizes a spectrum of valid perspectives. Both Billy and Jesse are outlaws, for example, but the way we view them is radically different. The former we condemn as a cold-blooded killer, the latter wins our sympathy in spite of his flaws. These things matter thanks to Bergon's artistry, his ability to tell compelling tales about authentic people and places we believe in and care about.

Works Cited

Bergon, Frank. "How to Know What to Write." Presentation at the Center of the American West, Boulder, CO. April 29, 2016.

———. *Jesse's Ghost*. Berkeley, CA.: Heyday, 2011.

———. "Rebellion in Marlboro Country." In *Two-Buck Chuck & The Marlboro Man: The New Old West*. Reno: University of Nevada Press, 2019.

———. *Shoshone Mike*. New York: Viking, 1987.

———. "The Search for Shoshone Mike." *Nevada Magazine* (November–December, 1987): 57-59.

———. *The Temptations of St. Ed & Brother S*. Reno: University of Nevada Press, 1993.

———. "The Toughest Kid We Knew." In *The Toughest Kid We Knew: The Old New West: A Personal History*. Reno: University of Nevada Press, 2020.

———. *Two-Buck Chuck & The Marlboro Man: The New Old West*. Reno: University of Nevada Press, 2019.

———. *Wild Game*. Reno: University of Nevada Press, 1995.

Coate, Bill. "Pieces of the Past." *Madera Tribune*. June 1, 2011

Heath, William. *The Children Bob Moses Led*. Minneapolis: Milkweed Editions, 1995.

Herman, Arthur. *How the Scots Invented the Modern World*. New York: Crown Publishing, 2001.

Long, Jeff. *Outlaw: The True Story of Claude Dallas*. New York: William Morrow, 1985.

Morris, Gregory L. *Frank Bergon*. Boise, ID: Boise State University, 1997.

Olson, Jack. *Give a Boy a Gun: A True Story of Law and Disorder*. New York: Delacorte Press, 1985.

Rio, David. "Basques in the International West: An Interview with Frank Bergon." *Western American Literature*. 36 (Spring 2001): 56-72.

Twain, Mark. *The Adventures of Huckleberry Finn*. Berkeley: University of California Press, 1985.

Warren, Robert Penn. *Selected Poems: New and Old 1923-1966*. New York: Random House, 1966.

Webb, James. *Born Fighting: How the Scots-Irish Shaped America*. New York: Broadway Books, 2004.

Fictive Truths: Frank Bergon's Literary Critique in a Post-Truth World

Sylvan Goldberg

Late in Herman Melville's *The Confidence-Man* (1857), the last novel Melville would publish before mostly abandoning prose fiction, the seemingly good-hearted but likely disingenuous Frank Goodman relates in brief the story of Charlemont, a merchant whose abrupt melancholic turn is followed soon after by the public announcement of his bankruptcy and his disappearance. Years later, Charlemont returns with his finances once again intact but with a lingering melancholy whose cause he refuses to reveal. If there is meaning to the story, it remains obscured—Frank insists he told it only "to amuse"—but of more pressing interest to its auditor is not meaning but truth: "A very strange one," Charlie insists, before asking Frank, "but is it true?"[1] Frank replies, "[o]f course not; if it seem strange to you, that strangeness is the romance; it is what contrasts it with real life; it is the invention, in brief, the fiction as opposed to the fact."[2] If Charlie's question puts a crack in the boundary between fact and fiction by highlighting the difficulty of knowing which we confront in the words of others, Frank's reply restabilizes that boundary by declaring "strangeness" its determining line.

These days, we might long for a world in which strangeness proves an indication of fictionality. Indeed, there is something distressingly familiar about the fictional world Melville creates aboard the *Fidèle*, the ship whose ironic name translates to faithful or true. In this second decade of the twenty-first-century United States—where a failed entrepreneur turned reality TV star inhabits the Oval Office, "alternative facts" are voiced on network news and then echo through the Twitterverse, and anti-science pundits and politicians have led a shocking number of Americans to disbelieve the mountains of scientific evidence of anthropogenic climate change—absurdity seems more a feature of reality than its opposite. And like the world Melville creates in *The Confidence-Man*, the blurred line between

---

1   Herman Melville, *The Confidence-Man* (1857; New York: The Modern Library, 2003), 212.
2   Ibid., 212.

fact and fiction opens up opportunities to undermine truth and to exploit the credulity of those around us. As truth has eroded under this pressure, our faith in the people with whom we share our world and the institutions that hold us together seems to have ebbed to a dismally low level, leading us into a "post-truth" moment whose motto might mirror that of the sign hung by the *Fidèle*'s barber: "No trust."[3] While this seems to have reached an apotheosis in the disingenuousness and outright lies of President Trump, the tension that anchors this moment, the disconnect between what one says or does and some stable truth behind those words or actions, stretches deep into American cultural history. Nancy Ruttenburg, whose concept of "democratic personality" seeks to understand the origins of American democracy through the performative power of public speech, traces this concept to the "apparent opposition . . . between an authentic trait of selfhood (who one is) and a performed or factitious one (how one acts)" that began in colonial New England with the Salem witch trials and the First Great Awakening.[4] Puritan culture marks a logical, albeit incomplete, starting point for much in American culture, and all the more so here, for the possibility remained baked into the Calvinist adherence to predestination that, as Edmund S. Morgan wrote in his classic account of the Puritan desire for a congregation made up only of the saved, "the leading of a holy life, was not . . . a strong enough sight to offer much comfort to poor, doubting Christians, for hypocrites could do good works."[5] We, too, like the Puritans and like the passengers aboard the *Fidèle*, wander through a world in which our external and internal selves can fail to align. But unlike the Puritans, we have gained the ability to sever that link ourselves—to turn selfhood into pure performance.

As Frank Bergon alerts us in a recent essay, these are questions of authenticity. In "Our Age of Sincere Inauthenticity," Bergon argues we have entered a moment in which "authenticity doesn't matter" and a performative version of selfhood unmoored from a "true" self dominates not just popular culture but the vast expanse of our social and political life.[6] The ingredients for such an age had been "bubbling in a cultural cauldron

3   Oxford Dictionaries named "post-truth" the 2016 word of year. See "Word of the Year 2016 is . . . ," Oxford University Press, accessed January 22, 2019, https://en.oxforddictionaries.com/word-of- the-year/word-of-the-year-2016.

4   Nancy Ruttenburg, *Democratic Personality: Popular Voice and the Trial of American Authorship* (Stanford: Stanford University Press), 8.

5   Edmund S. Morgan, *Visible Saints: The History of a Puritan Idea* (Ithaca: Cornell University Press, 1963), 67.

6   Frank Bergon. "Our Age of Sincere Inauthenticity," *Los Angeles Review of Books,* accessed May 15, 2020, https://lareviewofbooks.org/article/our-age-of-sincere-inauthenticity/.

. . . for some fifty years," but boiled over with the presidential election of Donald Trump, whose ability to ride his inauthenticity as a candidate into the White House ushered in an era of "sincere inauthenticity," full of public avowals of a dismissal of any cohesive self.[7] Such a world is not inherently a degraded one. Indeed, Bergon roams through a number of cultural moments and objects—Lionel Trilling's Vietnam-era Harvard lectures, later collected as *Sincerity and Authenticity*; boxing; Richard Prince's photographic reproductions; reality TV shows such as *American Idol*—to illuminate what he calls "the tragedy and necessity of human self-deception," which can undermine truth even as it opens up opportunities to redefine the self to which authenticity asks us to be true.[8] Positive engagement with such a perspective, however, necessitates a certain recognition and awareness, something the best of our current cultural moment evokes, while the worst equivocates: indeed, "[t]he question of Trump's awareness remains."[9] The post-truth era we inhabit, then, suspends us in a moment of interrogation—of others and ourselves—without resolution. The old Puritan anxieties return again, amplified through the technologies of social media and by a president who lays bare the crisis of the performative self that so recently offered to critical theory and to the cultural world writ large a site of resistance to the constraints of an oppressively vigilant normativity.

That Bergon has turned to these questions of authenticity at this late stage in his career emphasizes how central they have been to the writings—both creative and critical—that he has produced throughout his life. This is unsurprising for a novelist and scholar of the U.S. West, for questions of authenticity have animated the field of western American studies throughout its scholarly existence. As William Handley and Nathaniel Lewis argue, "there is no other region in America that is as haunted by the elusive appeal, legitimating power, and nostalgic pull of authenticity."[10] As they and other scholars of the U.S. West have shown, authenticity has been an organizing conceit in western studies in part because the region and the myth grew up together.[11] From the start, in a nation birthed through

---

7   Ibid.
8   Ibid.
9   Ibid.
10   William R. Handley and Nathaniel Lewis, "Introduction," in *True West: Authenticity and the American West*, ed. William R. Handley and Nathaniel Lewis (Lincoln: University of Nebraska Press, 2004), 1.
11   See, for example, Neil Campbell, *The Cultures of the New American West* (Edinburgh, Scotland: Edinburgh University Press, 2003); Nathaniel Lewis, *Unsettling the Literary West: Authenticity, Authorship, and Western American Literature* (Lincoln: University of Nebraska Press, 2003).

the textual mediation of founding documents such as the Declaration of Independence and the ideological labor of print culture and a reading public, the U.S. novel rose in tandem with the frontier spaces of a steadily shifting line demarcating the nation's West.[12] It did so self-consciously: as Charles Brockden Brown, considered by many the nation's first professional writer, would argue in his prefatory remarks to *Edgar Huntly; or Memoirs of a Sleep-Walker* (1799), literary effects and gothic affects were far better achieved with the contemporaneous American materials of "incidents of Indian hostility, and the perils of the Western wilderness" than with the historical orientation of the European gothic.[13] Thus, as early novelists like James Fenimore Cooper, Catherine Sedgwick, and Robert Montgomery Bird turned to the marginal spaces of the new nation, they hitched the American novel and its imaginative frontiers to the steadily moving line of the U.S. West. The fictional life of the new nation thus explored the same regions real-life explorers and settlers were simultaneously venturing into, raising questions of whose accounts were more accurate, more authentic—whose descriptions, in other words, could better represent truth.

Despite his own literary—as well as more literal—rambles through these same spaces, Bergon's scholarly writing remains less interested in pinning down the line between fact and fiction than in unpacking an epistemology built out of the relationship between the two. Across five decades of literary critique, Bergon has repeatedly examined the ties between imagination and material conditions in western American and environmental literature, presenting a vision of the United States in which fiction and fact operate in reciprocal relation to continually remake the world we inhabit. In the writings of two very different naturalists, the nature writer John Burroughs and the late-nineteenth-century novelist and short story writer Stephen Crane, and in the archives of wilderness literature and the literature of the U.S. West, Bergon brings to bear a vision of the world in which literature retains both ideological and material power. The written word, in Bergon's vision, responds to its environs, but remakes them as well. Given this, returning to Bergon's scholarly claims in the post-truth moment can tell us something about the anxieties of representation and reality in a moment where these two terms have grown so imbalanced they seem to have reversed their meaning, a moment in

---

12   On the relationship between a "national state [that] grounded its legitimacy . . . in the very special formation of print discourse," see Michael Warner, *The Letters of the Republic: Publication and the Public Sphere in Eighteenth-Century America* (Cambridge: Harvard University Press, 1990), xiv.

13   Charles Brockden Brown, *Edgar Huntly; or Memoirs of a Sleep-Walker* (1799; New York: Penguin, 1988), 3.

which representation more faithfully offers up something tangible and reality recedes ever further. Bergon's scholarly claims return again and again not just to the power of historical fact in shaping literary representation but to the ability of imagination to construct both historical knowledge and material spaces, spaces we have called wilderness, or the U.S. West—and often, in Bergon's writing, both at once.

These two terms—wilderness and the West—come together most explicitly in Bergon's dazzling and foundational account of the journals of Lewis and Clark. For Bergon, the journals encode the meeting of literary production and "an unfamiliar and often frightening wilderness," a world in which preconceptions and literary presumptions color the explorers' gaze, even as they collapse in an environment that challenges the "aesthetics of order, moderation, regularity, and stability [that] shaped [their] preconceptions of Western rivers and mountains."[14] As Bergon writes in his introduction to the Penguin edition of the excerpted journals, "[c] onventional rhetoric and cultural assumptions break down as the facts of the actual country, animals, and native peoples of the West give shape to new forms of perception."[15] The feedback loop here—inherited aesthetic value offers up a language and a structure that determines the way one sees the natural world, but the realities of that environment necessitate new ways of seeing and of describing, and thus shift aesthetic categories—registers a fundamental challenge of all nature writing, which seeks to translate into language a world that inherently escapes such limitations. All the more evident in unexplored regions where travelers encounter the unfamiliar, "[l]anguage itself," in the journals, "has to be altered to describe a new country and its native inhabitants; words coined and twisted and adapted to the occasion in the journals produced the addition of more than one thousand new words to the American language."[16]

The insufficiency of the imaginative and linguistic frames that Lewis and Clark brought west with them, and the need to expand these in response to an unfamiliar natural world, turns the journals, in Bergon's account, into an exemplary text for what scholars within the environmental humanities have more recently come to call material-discursive practices. A still-circulated, albeit reductively insufficient, explanation of the emergence

---

14   Frank Bergon, "Wilderness Aesthetics," *American Literary History* 9, no. 1 (Spring 1997): 46.
15   Frank Bergon, "Introduction," in *The Journals of Lewis and Clark*, ed. Frank Bergon (New York: Penguin, 1989), xviii.
16   Ibid., xviii.

of ecocriticism is that it came into being in and as a resistance to the dematerialization of the world wrought by poststructural critical theory.

Bergon's scholarly accounts of the natural world challenge such a narrative, for the privileging of language over matter, or vice versa, is absent from his discussions of the natural world. Rather, in his writings on Lewis and Clark, on wilderness, and on the naturalist John Burroughs, Bergon shows again and again the ways in which the perceptual lenses that shape our responses to the natural world are themselves reshaped by its intransigent matter. Bergon's accounts thus anticipate the recent emergence of material ecocriticism, which "[tries] to shed light on the way bodily natures and discursive forces *express* their interaction whether in representations or in their concrete reality."[17] What Donna Haraway has called "material-semiotic reality," or Kate Rigby, in her recent recoding of "natural disasters," refers to as "material-discursive processes," Bergon takes as his worldview beginning decades earlier.[18]

This understanding of the natural world as mediated through both the material and the discursive is perhaps most evident in Bergon's writings on John Burroughs, for whom "[l]ife is not just matter, and yet it cannot be separated from matter or the processes of the material world."[19] The cabin Burroughs built, Slabsides, and its environing woods remain a pilgrimage site in the Hudson Valley, a dozen or so miles upriver from Vassar College, Bergon's institutional home for much of his scholarly life. In Burroughs, Bergon seems to have found a writer whose geographic attachments added depth to Bergon's appreciation for a region far distant from the U.S. West that anchored so much of his creative writing. Burroughs depicts a lively world whose vibrancy aids our understanding, and Bergon illuminates this vitalism without resorting to the jargony language of much recent scholarship in the environmental humanities, telling us straightforwardly of Burroughs's environmental understanding "of nature as becoming . . . where there is no pause, no completion, no explanation."[20] Bergon's central reading of Burroughs sifts out an epistemology echoing his own—perhaps,

---

17   Serenella Iovino and Serpil Opperman, "Introduction: Stories Come to Matter," in *Material Ecocriticism*, ed. Serenella Iovino and Serpil Opperman (Bloomington: Indiana University Press, 2014), 2.

18   Donna Haraway, *The Donna Haraway Reader* (New York: Routledge, 2004), 2; Kate Rigby, *Dancing with Disaster: Environmental Histories, Narratives, and Ethics for Perilous Times* (Charlottesville: University of Virginia Press, 2015), 15.

19   Frank Bergon, "Introduction," in *A Sharp Lookout: Selected Nature Essays of John Burroughs*, ed. Frank Bergon (Washington, D.C.: Smithsonian Institution Press, 1987), 58.

20   Ibid., 31.

indeed, helping to form it—and laying bare the idea that a writer's task was not simply to record the world but to produce something otherwise unavailable. While "[i]t was solid reality Burroughs wanted in his own work," Bergon insists, the naturalist knew that "[f]or experience to become real it must pass through the imagination and the process of writing itself."[21] These are reassuring words for any writer, no doubt, but perhaps all the more so for a writer invested in the natural world, where "real" truth so often emerges through the claims of science. In Burroughs's work, the creative writer's ability to access a richer truth emerges in tandem with scientific fact rather than contrary to it, a tension Burroughs would draw out by castigating the anthropomorphism of the "nature fakers." It does so not just because subjective knowledge proves its own form of truth, as emotional content or the perceptual shifts wrought by figurative language. Rather, in Bergon's writings on Burroughs, the best of imaginative prose intervenes in the world, reshaping it through the productive power of the word. "Common facts and experiences are *changed*," Bergon writes, "and heightened according to the writer's quality of mind."[22]

It's a short leap from this view of imaginative writing's material effects and productive capabilities to a vision of writing itself as environmental activism, and so we find in Bergon's telling a Burroughs who rises to the level of environmentalist, anachronistic as the phrase may be. Though he notes "[a] widespread opinion about John Burroughs is that he was not a committed environmentalist, especially when compared to his western avatar and friend John Muir, who became a model for later nature writers advocating political action in defense of threatened wilderness areas," Bergon was more narrowly defending his muse from the criticisms of Bill McKibben, who had "nearly transform[ed] the naturalist into an antienvironmentalist" in an essay in the *New York Review of Books* (later reprinted, as Bergon alerts us, "as the introduction to [McKibben's] Penguin edition of [Burroughs's] *Birch Browsings*").[23] Not shy about picking this fight— he calls McKibben's claims "quarter-truths"—Bergon argues that Burroughs proves his environmentalist chops not despite but because of the ways in which he shifts environmental attention away from the exploration and wilderness narratives to which Bergon himself had earlier attended: "from Burroughs we learn that the real trek of discovery consists not in

---

21   Ibid., 12, 35.
22   Ibid., 33; emphasis added.
23   Frank Bergon, " 'Sensitive to the Verge of the Horizon': The Environmentalism of John Burroughs," in *Sharp Eyes: John Burroughs and American Nature Writing*, ed. Charlotte Zoë Walker (Syracuse: Syracuse University Press, 2000), 19.

exploring new landscapes but in having new eyes."[24] Indeed, Burroughs becomes not simply an environmentalist *avant la lettre*, but an anticipator of theorizations of the Anthropocene, the recently coined term for the geologic epoch in which humans have irreversibly altered earth systems. Unsurprisingly, given Bergon's repeated returns to questions of authenticity and of artifice, these ideas emerge out of Burroughs's "idea about the destructive artifice of modern life, [which,] planted in his journal in 1866, matured years later into his dire reflection in 1912 that the time may be coming when man's scientific knowledge, and the 'vast system of artificial things with which it has enabled him to surround himself, [will] cut short his history upon the planet.' "[25]

What *is* surprising, because the bulk of his scholarship was published before theorizations of this new geological epoch, is that Bergon, too, emerges as a necessary and neglected figure in Anthropocene critique. In his turn to genre as a tool for understanding the journals of Lewis and Clark, he offers up a useful corrective to cultural accounts of the Anthropocene that focus on content rather than on the formal structures that have produced such apocalyptic material circumstances.[26] Bergon's true innovation in his account of the journals is to view them not simply as an expression of the reciprocal relationship between word and world, as discussed above, but as an imaginative encounter that sets a course for American literature, and for the nation itself: "[t]hese uneven, fragmented, and unpolished journals offered the equivalent of a national poem, a magnificent epic for an unfinished nation."[27] This epic quality lends them a productive power, an ability to engender the nation they sung. And yet, the nation they spawned has failed to take their lessons. Bergon, unafraid to moralize at times in his own writing, performs the role of Jeremiah at the conclusion of his introduction to the Penguin edition, seeing the denuded world in which he writes as a failure to retain the epic vision of which the journals sing: "the real snake in the garden hideously follows the explorers themselves," writes Bergon. "In the wanton smashing

---

24   Ibid., 24.
25   Ibid., 21.
26   Recently, literary scholars have begun similarly to advance a reckoning with the formal questions raised by the Anthropocene. For the place of genre, in particular, in this conversation, see Stephanie LeMenager, "Climate Change and the Struggle for Genre," in *Anthropocene Reading: Literary History in Geologic Times*, ed. Tobias Menely and Jesse Oak Taylor (University Park: Pennsylvania State University Press, 2017), 220-238.
27   Frank Bergon, "The Journals of Lewis and Clark: An American Epic," in *Old West—New West: Centennial Essays*, ed. Barbara Howard Meldrum (Moscow: University of Idaho Press, 1993), 134.

of a wolf's skull with a spontoon, the slaughtering of animals and the proprietary attitudes toward the land and native peoples, we get sad glimpses of the coming dark side of American imperialism."[28] We can read this, with Bergon, as a refusal of the journals' appreciation of the natural world of the United States. But instead, the lesson we might take from Bergon's turn to the language of genre to discuss the journals is a recognition that the Anthropocene names not merely a geologic epoch or an awareness of environmental harm, but a reorientation of our environmental encounters as predicated on the ways genre trains us to read. For it is repetition and reinforcement more than sublime exceptionality that structure the bulk of our interactions with the natural world, just like it is the repetitions of harmful environmental practices that have sent us hurtling toward the catastrophes of climate change. The generic quality of these behaviors—everything from the perpetual motion of oil derricks to the cellophane-wrapped fruits and vegetables that line bodega shelves across Manhattan—produces the scaled-up harm that the Anthropocene seeks to understand. That our recognition of the harm stemming from these repetitions has emerged so belatedly only adds to the power of Bergon's invocation of genre, a literary concept whose validity can only ever be named after it has coalesced.

Discussions of genre return us to Bergon's work on the U.S. West, if only because the central questions evoked by genre—of repetition and recurrence; of type and anti-type—help us to see what Bergon resists in his account of the West. Bergon tends to skip past the conventional genre western, or what he sometimes calls the "horse opera," in favor of texts whose western imagination adheres more closely to his understanding of the relationship between representation and region: the "real" West as it engages the mythic West. Indeed, "[t]he American West," write Bergon and Zeese Papanikolas in the preface to *Looking Far West*, their collection of western American literature, "surely created myths, but myths themselves just as surely created the West," which was "an intricate combination of both myth and reality."[29] This interest runs throughout Bergon's novelistic takes on the West, and his scholarly discussions, too, seek out when and where these two Wests meet.

Echoing the aesthetic manifestos of Americans across the nineteenth century—Charles Brockden Brown, as we have seen, but also the painter

---

28 Bergon, "Introduction," in *The Journals*, xviii–xix.
29 Frank Bergon and Zeese Papanikolas, "General Introduction," in *Looking Far West*, ed. Frank Bergon and Zeese Papanikolas (New York: New American Library, 1978), 2.

Thomas Cole and the novelist and critic Frank Norris—Bergon and Papanikolas insist that "[t]he country had no past, but it did have a West, a faraway, romantic place that could serve as a basis for myth."[30] Like his account of the journals of Lewis and Clark, Bergon describes the West here not through its traditional generic affiliation—not, that is, through the conventions of the western, with its cowboys, sheriffs, and outlaws, its shootouts and horseback chases—but as "an epic that did not exist in one poem or in several, or in one historical moment or another, but in a consciousness and a yonder."[31] While those "mythic figures offered Westerners something to live up to," engendering character types that leaked off the page, the true constitutive power of the West as concept lies in the different generic affiliation Bergon and Papanikolas evoke in calling it an epic.[32] The story the western tells, the one Bergon himself repeats throughout his scholarly work, is one that lies at the heart of the epic: the ability to call forth a nation, to forge a foundational myth whose material effects and importance to the history of the United States extend far beyond the capabilities of the western genre. "As attractive as the legendary West is in its simplicity," Bergon insists, "it cannot satisfy our sense of the historical West."[33]

This account of the West anchors Bergon's readings of Stephen Crane, whose western writings, collected by Bergon in the aptly titled *The Western Writings of Stephen Crane*, "give us glimpses of historical complexities that the fantasies of most horse operas cannot support."[34] Crane stands out among Bergon's subjects, and for good reason: wide-ranging despite his short life, Crane's variety of genre, style, and subject makes him a challenging writer for critics to pin down. Bergon's masterly book-length take on Crane's "habit of imagination," in *Stephen Crane's Artistry* (1975), remains a necessary citation for any Crane scholar, and it culminates with a chapter on what Bergon calls Crane's "suitable subject," the American West. Crane, influenced by earlier western writers such as Bret Harte, Mark Twain, and the more fanciful dime novels but writing in a moment that preceded the modern western, "wrote anti-Westerns before the Western became a formula" through the works that followed on the heels of Owen Wister's *The Virginian* (1902) and Zane Grey's *Riders of the Purple*

---

30   Ibid., 8.
31   Ibid.
32   Ibid., 10.
33   Frank Bergon, "Introduction," in *The Western Writings of Stephen Crane*, ed. Frank Bergon (New York: Signet, 1979), 5.
34   Ibid., 5.

Sage (1912).[35] But while Crane was more faithful than later western writers to historical reality, and more willing to ironize romantic archetypes, his western stories exemplify the insufficiency of what I earlier described as "two Wests," for myth and reality prove mutually constitutive, each shifting in response to the other: "Nor could a simple division between 'myth' and 'reality' accommodate Crane's more profound understanding of the actual West, for he was one of the few writers in the late nineteenth century to recognize how the myth of the West had become part of its historical reality."[36] Stories like "The Bride Comes to Yellow Sky" may "[banish] the purely legendary West to the realm of fantasy," but they "[affirm] the role of that fantasy in creating the historical West."[37] In Bergon's hands, then, Crane becomes like Lewis and Clark in their journals, or Burroughs in his nature writing: "For Crane, experience must be transformed, and in the process language itself is transformed."[38] We see, then, in the recurrence of this central thread of Bergon's critique, a worldview we can ascribe to Bergon himself, which appears time and again, and in whomever and whatever Bergon casts his scholarly gaze upon. It is an account of literature's place in the world that sees in fiction the power to make fact, to body forth a world off the page. As Bergon writes of Crane's "The Blue Hotel," "the mythical Wild West often became reality in unexpected places because its true locale was a country in the mind."[39]

As this account of the West as a "country in the mind" emphasizes, Crane's representations render him the exemplar of Bergon's understanding of the co-constitutive relationship between fact and fiction. Bergon insists that "[f]or Crane the 'real thing' often seems not to be somewhere awaiting his discovery but rather the creation of his imagination, wrenched into existence."[40] This interest in imagination emphasizes what Crane takes true aim at in his fiction: the ways in which moments of subjective experience force us to recognize the failure of our attempts to reach some final, objective truth or reality. Filtered through what Bergon calls Crane's "transformative imagination," the world seems continually to shift around Crane's characters, showing us "not so much observed reality as reality metamorphosed."[41] It is a strikingly modern account of the world

---

35   Ibid., 2.
36   Ibid., 10.
37   Ibid., 11.
38   Frank Bergon, *Stephen Crane's Artistry* (New York: Columbia University Press, 1975), 28.
39   Ibid., 131.
40   Ibid., xi.
41   Ibid., 34, 31.

for a writer still attached to the romance that had dominated American literature throughout the nineteenth century, "reproduc[ing] a modern equivocal view of reality."[42] Such a perspective risks undermining the stability not just of Truth, with a capital T, but of moral action, for "[i]n such a world of shifting meanings, there can be no certain understanding or moral judgment," and we see here the ways in which Bergon's account of Crane anticipates the crisis of the post-truth age.[43] For in rendering truth equivocal and meaning unstable while remaining committed to a vision of the world in which the imagination retains productive power in the material realm, Crane cracks open the possibility that we might act in a moment of misjudgment and so effect a world produced through misinterpretation. These "misperception[s] can produce actions so influential to a situation that the false perception becomes a true one," that, in other words, actions can produce a world where, rather than remaining open, meaning remakes itself in a singular, and singularly bad, form.[44] Meaning making, in other words, necessitates the ability to maintain the power of imagination without losing the ability to see things as they are.

Much of the anxiety of the Trump era emerges from the exploitation of these instabilities of meaning, a type of bad poststructuralism that renders all truth equivocal at the service of advancing a lie. This has not gone unnoticed in academia. As Christopher Schaberg writes in *The Work of Literature in an Age of Post-Truth*, "in some corners of academia right now, there is a feeling of defeat and acceptance at what is seen as an appropriation of theoretical tactics applied to regressive politics."[45] And yet, there is a certain irony in Trump's emblematic status as poststructural politics' apotheosis, for postmodernism's attachment to the liberalism of late capitalism seems rather to make Trump, given his attachment to authoritarianism, its anti-avatar. Trump's espousal of alternative facts does not shift the frame to encompass a pluralism of meaning. It remains at the service of one overriding truth claim, and usually a false one, to which Trump remains committed. The outright lies of the supposed post-truth era thus return us to a world in which Truth remains capitalized and singular. From the social production of meaning, we now return to the individual: Trump as meaning maker. While the post-truth world seems to broaden the influence of poststructuralism, it in fact restricts it. For

---

42   Ibid., 65.
43   Ibid., 24.
44   Ibid., 41.
45   Christopher Schaberg, *The Work of Literature in an Age of Post-Truth* (New York: Bloomsbury, 2018), 11.

Schaberg, this necessitates a return to the perspectivism that subtends a more faithful poststructural account of the world, a recognition that "the more perspectives we are able to draw together, the more comprehensive our objectivity will be," producing "an openness to extra-subjective imagination that can spur empathy with respect to others."[46]

Crane, and Bergon, offer us a similar way out, but one that shifts the onus off of the other, a move so often critiqued in a moment where the challenges of decentering whiteness and the patriarchal establishment—two power structures that anchor Trump's presidency—have put a great deal of intellectual and emotional labor on the backs of those who inhabit minoritized identity positions. For Crane, an individual's perspective is already split into the multiple vantages of perspectivalism, and he "diverts both his readers and himself from packaging the mysteries of reality, he prevents singleness of vision by insuring multiple perspectives."[47] If authenticity registers an alignment of exterior and interior in some stable and consistent way, Crane helps us to see the ways in which such an alignment can never truly come into being. This does, as Schaberg insists, ask us to recognize the other as one aspect of the world's multiplicity of meaning, and therefore to try to take their perspective into account. But it also necessitates an ability to take our own multiplicity into account, to gain self-knowledge but not singular truth. This is, in part, what Bergon asks of us in his recent essay on sincere inauthenticity. Writing of Oscar Wilde's stylized mode of moving through the world, Bergon says, "[a] century after Wilde advised the young to be as artificial as possible, he might now say that their second duty is to be, as he was, aware of it."[48] For, "[i]f awareness grants freedom, then recognition of inauthenticity and self-deception may perhaps free us to become less so."[49] What emerges, then, is less a question of authenticity than a search for a mode of inhabitation more faithful to a reframing of reality, one concerned less with aligning internal and external— subjective and objective—than with recognizing the ways in which the relationship between our ever-shifting interior life and the material world we inhabit has genuine consequences. In arguing throughout his scholarly career that our imaginations have the power to remake a world constantly remaking our selves and our imaginations, Bergon has shown in the way in which questions of the self are questions of the world.

---

46   Ibid., 11.
47   Bergon, *Stephen Crane's Artistry*, 146.
48   Ibid.
49   Bergon, "Our Age."

In a 1998 essay detailing his travels in the Chiapas region of Mexico, the geographic heart of the Zapatista movement, Bergon anchors his essay—like his travels—in a search for "La Realidad—the Zapatista village ... [and] headquarters of Subcomandante Marcos, the ski-masked, pipe-smoking multilingual leader of the 1994 peasant uprising."[50] Fully aware of the pun that anchors his essay—which, after all, he titles "Come with Me to Reality"—Bergon ranges through the multiple stakeholders and perspectives the uprising engages, acknowledging throughout the material impact of these competing interests on the Mexican land in "a conflict that is fundamentally environmental."[51] But if the essay opens with the idea that Reality, La Realidad, is a stable place—a city somewhere in the Lacandón jungle—that Bergon might reach, by essay's end, he makes clear that reality is the journey itself, the process of moving through these multiple perspectives and the irresolution endemic to doing so. If a post-truth world contains the power to open up meaning and remake our world in better terms—or rather, *through* better terms—we can do so only by seeing the monomania of a figure like Trump not as post-truth's apotheosis but as its opposite, as a figuration of the destructive power of refusing the intersecting multiplicities that emanate out from each of us. Crane makes clear how challenging it can be to locate oneself in such a vision of the world we inhabit, in which beliefs can shift from moment to moment, sentence to sentence. And yet, "we still have to get to Reality," Bergon insists to his traveling companion at the end of his essay on the Zapatistas. Her reply, one Bergon has been repeating to us throughout his scholarly career, stands as the only stable truth in the slippery remakings of the post-truth world: "We're there, babe."[52]

---

50 Frank Bergon, "Come with Me to Reality," *Terra Nova: Journal of Nature and Culture* 3, no. 1 (Winter 1998): 17.
51 Ibid.
52 Ibid., 34

WORKS CITED

Bergon, Frank. "Come with Me to Reality." *Terra Nova: Journal of Nature and Culture* 3, no. 1 (Winter 1998): 16-34.

————. "Introduction." In *The Journals of Lewis and Clark*, edited by Frank Bergon, ix–xix. New York: Penguin, 1989.

————. "Introduction." In *A Sharp Lookout: Selected Nature Essays of John Burroughs*, edited by Frank Bergon, 9–64. Washington, D.C.: Smithsonian Institution Press, 1987.

————. "Introduction." In *The Western Writings of Stephen Crane*, edited by Frank Bergon, 1-27. New York: Signet, 1979.

————. "The Journals of Lewis and Clark: An American Epic." In *Old West— New West: Centennial Essays*, edited by Barbara Howard Meldrum, 133–45. Moscow: University of Idaho Press, 1993.

————. "Our Age of Sincere Inauthenticity," *Los Angeles Review of Books*. Accessed May 15, 2020. https://lareviewofbooks.org/article/our-age-of-sincere-inauthenticity.

————. " 'Sensitive to the Verge of the Horizon': The Environmentalism of John Burroughs." In *Sharp Eyes: John Burroughs and American Nature Writing*, edited by Charlotte Zoë Walker, 19–25. Syracuse: Syracuse University Press, 2000.

————. *Stephen Crane's Artistry*. New York: Columbia University Press, 1975.

————. "Wilderness Aesthetics." *American Literary History* 9, no. 1 (Spring 1997): 128–161.

Bergon, Frank and Zeese Papanikolas. "General Introduction." In *Looking Far West*, edited by Frank Bergon and Zeese Papanikolas, 1-14. New York: New American Library, 1978.

Brown, Charles Brockden. *Edgar Huntly; or Memoirs of a Sleep-Walker*. 1799. New York: Penguin, 1988.

Campbell, Neil. *The Cultures of the New American West*. Edinburgh, Scottland: Edinburgh University Press, 2003.

Handley, William R. and Nathaniel Lewis. "Introduction." In *True West: Authenticity and the American West*, edited by William R. Handley and Nathaniel Lewis, 1-17. Lincoln: University of Nebraska Press, 2004.

Haraway, Donna. *The Donna Haraway Reader*. New York: Routledge, 2004.

Iovino, Serenella and Serpil Opperman. "Introduction: Stories Come to Matter." In *Material Ecocriticism*, edited by Serenella Iovino and Serpil Opperman, 1-17. Bloomington: Indiana University Press, 2014.

LeMenager, Stephanie. "Climate Change and the Struggle for Genre." In *Anthropocene Reading: Literary History in Geologic Times*, edited by Tobias Menely and Jesse Oak Taylor, 220-38. University Park: Pennsylvania State University Press, 2017.

Lewis, Nathaniel. *Unsettling the Literary West: Authenticity, Authorship, and Western American Literature*. Lincoln: University of Nebraska Press, 2003.

Melville, Herman. *The Confidence-Man*. 1857, New York: The Modern Library, 2003.

Morgan, Edmund S. *Visible Saints: The History of a Puritan Idea*, Ithaca: Cornell University Press, 1963.

Rigby, Kate. *Dancing with Disaster: Environmental Histories, Narratives, and Ethics for Perilous Times*. Charlottesville: University of Virginia Press, 2015.

Ruttenburg, Nancy. *Democratic Personality: Popular Voice and the Trial of American Authorship*. Stanford: Stanford University Press, 1998.

Schaberg, Christopher. *The Work of Literature in an Age of Post-Truth*. New York: Bloomsbury, 2018.

Warner, Michael. *The Letters of the Republic: Publication and the Public Sphere in Eighteenth-Century America*. Cambridge: Harvard University Press, 1990.

"Word of the Year 2016 is . . ." Oxford University Press. Accessed January 22, 2019. https://en.oxforddictionaries.com/word-of-the-year/word-of-the-year-2016.

Frank Bergon's Papers:
A Multifaceted Archival Collection

Iñaki Arrieta Baro

The Frank Bergon Literary and Pictorial Collection gathers the papers, pictures, and manuscripts generated and compiled by Frank Bergon during his career. Besides giving us an insider's view of the development of Frank's works, it provides us with the opportunity to explore the connections among his multicultural family and literary network. This chapter aims to describe the contents of the collection available at the Jon Bilbao Basque Library and the archival processing implemented during 2018.

In September of 2017, Joseba Zulaika, Professor at the William A. Douglass Center for Basque Studies (CBS), contacted the Jon Bilbao Basque Library in regards to Frank Bergon. Joseba was enthusiastic about Frank's work and informed us that he was interested in donating his archival collection. Joseba suggested that I contact Frank directly and work on bringing his papers to Reno.

At the time, I knew little about Frank Bergon or his work. I remembered an article published in *Euskonews* some years ago and a presentation by Monika Madinabetia during the CBS's seminar series, but not much else. However, with each reading about him, my interest in the collection increased.

The Basque Library's mission is to gather all kinds of documentation related to the Basque Diaspora to serve as a memory institution of Basque Americans; our collection policy states that "Collections (papers, photographs, multimedia) related to the Diaspora (family, personal, institutional) and the various exiles in the Americas" fall within our remit. Thus, it was clear from the start that the archival collection of a Basque Nevada author and researcher such as Frank Bergon was of interest. Talking with Frank, we were able to assess that this interest was reciprocal, which is crucial for any donation to happen: he wanted his papers to reside in

Reno and be made available to researchers at the Basque Library. That being clear, we involved other units of the library and Kathy Ray, Dean of Libraries, in the conversation about how to house the donation of the collection in the Basque Library.

This conversation included talking about rights, access restrictions, contents, and so on. Size is a critical factor when an archival repository faces the donation of a collection since the number of documents greatly impacts the ability to process them. The expected size of the collection at the time was 20 cubic feet. After the first three transfers of documentation, we expect the collection to include up to 50 cubic feet of documents.

After various meetings, messages, and phone calls, in October 2017 Frank and the University Libraries signed the deed of gift and the Frank Bergon Literary and Pictorial collection was formally donated to the Jon Bilbao Basque Library.

During the conversation previous to the donation, one of the points we talked about was how to name the collection. According to *Describing Archives: A Content Standard, Second Edition* or DACS, the standard for describing archival collections in use in North American repositories, "titles generally have two parts:

- the name of the creator(s) or collector(s)
- the nature of the materials being described"

In our case, the first part was quite clear: Frank Bergon is the creator of the collection. From my point of view, the second part was also manifest. Again, according to DACS: "2.3.19 Archival materials are frequently described by devised aggregate terms such as papers (for personal materials), records (for organizational materials), or collection (for topical aggregations)."

Based on this definition, the title that I proposed for the collection was *Frank Bergon Papers*. This title reflects a standard way to identify a manuscript collection. However, Frank had another idea in mind, and he proposed the title *Frank Bergon Literary and Pictorial Collection*.

This title was finally chosen, among other reasons, because it is a good indication for anyone approaching the collection of its contents: of the 36 boxes received during 2018 by the Basque Library, 12 contain photographs, a third of the total. This variety is also reflected in the type of physical form of the documents, since the collection includes paper documents, both texts and photographs, video and audio recordings, as well as digital contents:

- Manuscripts and related materials of research and literary works
    o Research materials
    o Drafts
    o Printing proofs
    o Unpublished texts and chapters
- Paperwork related to the publishing process
    o Proposals
    o Letters to and from publishers
    o Contracts
    o Marketing materials
    o Publication catalogs
- Published monographs (2 boxes)
    o One circulating copy
    o One non-circulating archival copy
- Teaching materials (1 box)
- Correspondence (1 box)
- Pictures (10 boxes)
    o Family photos
        ▪ Nuclear family
        ▪ Collected images of the extended Basque and Béarnaise family
    o Personal life pictures
        ▪ Boyhood photos
        ▪ High School and college photos
    o Professional life
        ▪ Research related photographs
        ▪ Meeting and conferences
        ▪ Talks and readings
- Posters and oversized materials (2 boxes)

Besides the photograph series, there are also pictures in other parts of the collection, as in the case of Shoshone Mike's research materials, among which we can find historical photographs related to the events that are reflected in the novel.

The first step of archival processing is the acquisition of the newly arrived materials. The acquisition includes checking that the contents of the storage units—being boxes, folders, or hard drives, and so on—match the contents described in lists, inventories, or any other descriptive tool provided by the donor. This first step of the process is completed, and the acquisition of the 36 cubic feet has been transferred to the library.

The next step is to rehouse the materials, which involves storing the documents in archival quality folders, boxes, and other types of preservation materials adequate to guarantee their optimal conservation. Most of the paper documents and audio or video recordings are already transferred to this type of storage. We are now halfway through the process in the case of photographs.

The arrangement of the collection is, according to DACS, "[t]he process of organizing materials with respect to their provenance and original order, to protect their context and to achieve physical or intellectual control over the materials." We follow the principle of respecting the original order of the creator of the collection. There are situations in which the archivist could decide to make changes to the arrangement of the documents to make them more accessible or easier to understand. In the case of the Bergon Collection, these changes have been minimal, mostly related to the physical order of folders in storage boxes, not to the intellectual order of the collection.

The proposed arrangement of the collection maintains, for the most part, the order we found at the transfer. Even if, with the next arrival of materials, some changes might be expected, these would be minimal:

- One series for each main work
  - *Shoshone Mike*
  - *The Temptations of St. Ed & Brother S*
  - *Wild Game*
  - *Jesse's Ghost*
  - *The Western Writings of Stephen Crane*
  - *The Wilderness Reader*
  - *Nature Essays of John Burroughs*
  - [...]
- Essays and Reviews
- Readings, Talks, Activism
- Correspondence

- Basque topics
- Personal and family life

Specific materials—recordings and photographs—could be separated from the main physical collection, while maintaining their original provenance and order. Additionally, digital materials will be processed according to their particular needs, but, again, keeping the unity of the whole collection.

The archival processing, including description, is now finished for two series: *Shoshone Mike* and Correspondence. Some questions still need to be clarified with Frank regarding the sections on Basque topics and "Readings, Talks, Activism." Our goal now is to finish the processing of the materials transferred to the library; after that, we will plan the processing of digital materials in the collection and continue the conversation with Frank regarding pending materials.

The availability of the collection for researchers and the general public is a huge step forward to interpret the work of a critical author in Basque American literature. The Frank Bergon Literary and Pictorial Collection provides access to thousands of documents (drafts, notes, letters, and interviews), pictures, and recordings generated by and related to Frank Bergon. Opening up the materials of the Frank Bergon Collection creates new research opportunities to better understand Frank, the researcher, Frank, the author, and Frank, the Basque American Westerner.

Apocalypse and Transfiguration in Nevada's Nuclear Test Site: Frank Bergon's Desert of the Real

Joseba Zulaika

Frank Bergon's compelling novel *The Temptations of St. Ed & Brother S* confronts the reader with this radical alternative: "You either have faith in the mushroom cloud or in the Cloud of the Unknowing [a mystical text from the Middle Ages]."[1] The choice is best articulated in the two epigraphs to chapter 12, entitled "The Feast of the Transfiguration." The first one is from Matthew 7:1-3, words from the gospel read in the Catholic liturgy on August 6, the day of the Feast of the Transfiguration: "Six days later, Jesus took Peter, James, and John the brother of James, and led them up a high mountain where they were alone: and in their presence he was transfigured—his face shone like the sun, and his clothes became white as light." The second quote is from a survivor of the Hiroshima bombing: "Hiroshima: Monday morning at 8:15, August 6, 1945. It was a very fine day. Suddenly like a flashbulb going off, a kind of blue covered the entire city. Smoke and fire twisted as if reaching all the way to heaven. Black rain fell."[2] This is the apocalyptic alternative in Bergon's text that deals with the religious and political dilemmas of activist monks who combine desert spirituality and antinuclear protest.

The novel is situated in a hermitage in the middle of Nevada's desert where the 49-year-old Cistercian Trappist monk known as St. Ed, whose real name is Edward St. John Arrizabalaga, dreams of carrying a monastic life in the company of a young novitiate, Brother S, a former lumberjack from Oregon who keeps the solar-powered compound functioning while expecting a mystical experience. "Oh no," Abbot Arrizabalaga tells the

---

1   Bergon, *The Temptations of St. Ed & Brother S* (Reno: University of Nevada Press, 1993), 191.
2   Ibid., 185.

novice, "we don't have visions here." He even orders him, "I don't want you reading those mystics anymore."[3] To the abbot's question of why he wanted to be in the monastery, Brother S answered, "to be a saint." Arrizabalaga growls at the suggestion of sainthood: "What is this? What is this arrogance, this shitty self-centeredness, this pride?"[4] The monks try to emulate the desert fathers of the fourth century while carrying for sale to the neighboring towns of Tonopah and Warm Springs cases of Hermitage Honey.

Where does Frank Bergon get this idea of the religious enclave in the middle of the Nevada desert? It came from his own brother, who had found one such place there. In the novel the monastery is lost in the middle of nowhere, except there is something in the vicinity—Nevada's Nuclear Test Site. And there is on the horizon a bright city for these two celibate men—Las Vegas. Las Vegas is, of course, America's emblematic city where, down the Strip in the area called Paradise, Donald Trump has his 64-story Tower, with its gold-infused windows and gigantic gold-plated letters TRUMP at its top rising above the other buildings. Here you can find Fitzgerald's Great Gatsby and the "colossal vitality of his illusion"[5] reactivated by Trump's presidency. Fitzgerald's hard-boiled novel is the story "of a national 'shipwreck' that's looming on the outer edge."[6] He appears a captive of Fate, not its master. Fitzgerald tried to explain to a friend that "the whole burden of this novel—[is] the loss of those illusions that give such color to the world that you don't care whether things are true or false as long as they partake of the magical glory."[7] Such is the power of dreams at the nexus of Las Vegas and the NTS/Creech Air Base, neon lights and drone technologies, which "renders the American Dream irresistible and heartbreaking and buoyant, all at once."[8]

Las Vegas is also the city of Hunter Thompson's *Fear and Loathing in Las Vegas*, a novel read by one of Bergon's characters in the book. Thompson's novel is about its two Gonzo protagonists' "savage journey to the heart of the American Dream." Duke's attorney in Thompson's novel says to a waitress in Las Vegas: "Let me explain it to you . . . We're looking for the American Dream . . . All we were told was, go till you find

3   Ibid., 5, 8.
4   Ibid., 9.
5   F. Scott Fitzgerald, *The Great Gatsby* (New York: Scribner, 1925), 95.
6   Maureen Corrigan, *So We Read On: How the Great Gatsby Came to Be and Why It Endures* (New York: Little, Brown, 2014), 149.
7   Quoted in Corrigan, *So We Read*, 169.
8   Ibid., 175.

the American Dream. Take this white Cadillac and go find the American Dream. It's somewhere in the Las Vegas area."[9]

Las Vegas is the city of mirages with a time warp, where you regress to the Second World War, Cold War, Nuclear War, Vietnam War, War on Terror, Drone War, where you are propelled to future wars of fantastic technologies and apocalyptic terror, where a Great Military Barrack is married to a Great Whore. "Awww, mama . . . can this really . . . be the end . . . ?" Dylan sings in his "Memphis Blues Again." Steven Paddock might have been listening to Dylan while on October 1, 2017, he rained rapid-fired bullets from the 32nd-story room in the Mandalay Hotel-Casino on people in the outdoor music festival below, killing 58 and injuring 900 others. The man squeezing the trigger was also an emblem of the American Dream, one sung by John Lennon as "Happiness *is* a warm gun."

Trump's Las Vegas is the contemporary equivalent of Fitzgerald's colossal fantasies in *The Great Gatsby*. And Thompson's delirious Las Vegas novel is the contemporary equivalent of the delirious youth culture of the 1960s and 1970s, touching on the hidden core of American dreaming. But Frank Bergon had a different idea. His ambitious novel tells us that if you want a true landscape of America, one that competes with Fitzgerald's and Thompson's, you must journey first to Las Vegas but then go on north 65 miles on Highway 95 to the Nevada Test Site, and there you can find in all its power and apocalypse the true measure of the American Dream.

The task is how to conceptualize the dynamic of mutual denial and mutual constitution between these two transfigurations—the mushroom cloud and the mystical cloud of love to which Bergon's characters are committed. "We reject the energy of death and waste," says Arrizabalaga. "We choose the vital energy of love—I'm not just preaching away up here—I'm talking about the all-consuming energy of love."[10] The interplay of these two cloud alternatives displays the qualities of the psychoanalytic notion of *the edge*—"a duality that has nothing to do with the dichotomies between complementary oppositional terms . . . the edge is the thing whose only substantiality consists in its simultaneously separating and linking two surfaces . . . a duality that simultaneously constitutes the cause, the advent, and the consequences of the Real."[11] It is America's duality as a Christian nation ready to enact an apocalypse on the basis of its national fetish,

9   Hunter Thompson, *Fear and Loathing in Las Vegas* (New York: Vintage, 1998), 164-165.
10 *Temptations*, 191.
11 Alenca Zupancic, *The Shortest Shadow: Nietzsche's Philosophy of the Two* (Cambridge: MIT Press, 2003),19.

the Bomb. Bergon's novel is about the apocalyptic dilemmas of nuclear America in the 1980s, a predicament that is as urgent today as it was then. It is a sustained effort to grasp the radicalness of the "non-relationship" at the edge of these two transfigurations.

The Desert of the Real and the Force of Fantasy

One thing the novelist knows is the overpowering power of fantasy in human affairs. Bergon's monk St. Ed Arrizabalaga was most conscious of the force of fantasy in American life when he said that "fantasy . . . was what . . . made America go around . . . If all the energy generated by American fantasies in one minute could be harnessed," St. Ed maintained, "the cities of the world would have power for a hundred years . . . The result was the most shallow sense of reality human beings had ever had in history."[12]

In the 1999 film *The Matrix* by the Wachowski brothers, the hero awakens from a computer-generated virtual reality into the really real to see a desolate landscape of burned ruins, while the hero of the resistance greets him with, "Welcome to the desert of the real!" The expression is taken from Jean Baudrillard, who wrote that if Jorge Luis Borges could write a fable in which the cartographers of the Empire made a map so detailed that it covered the entire territory exactly, now "[i]t is the real, and not the map, whose vestiges subsist here and there, in the deserts which are no longer those of the Empire, but our own: The desert of the real itself."[13] Zizek applied the phrase "Welcome to the desert of the real" to analyze the events of 9/11: if the terrorist "passion for the Real" ended up in a kind of spectacle, inversely the postmodern passion for semblance ends up in the encounter with the real, as America with 9/11 got what it had fantasized in the Hollywood movies.[14]

Bergon locates the dialectics between the simulacrum and the real in the actual Nevada desert. He doesn't need any dystopian *Matrix*-like landscape in the midst of a virtual world. He has his desert of the real at home. The novel's landscape is desert America with its emptiness and silence, with highways as distant vanishing points for speeding and

---

12 *Temptations*, 125.
13 Jean Baudrillard, *Simulacra and Simulation* (Ann Arbor: University of Michigan Press, 1994), 1.
14 Slavoj Zizek, *Welcome to the Desert of the Real* (New York: Wooster Press, 2001), 16-17.

disappearing, and with occasional motels and gas stations by the road. At its heart is the endless military complex Nellis Air Base, almost as large as Israel or Belgium, Area 51 its secret spot, the Nuclear Test Site the location for the fetish Bomb, on its horizon Las Vegas a mirage of the sublime.

But is this place of fantasies real, or is it rather a *Dreamland*, the military's other name for Area 51? It is the desert of the real for the American military empire. And so is it for the thousands who died from plutonium fallout. But Baudrillard wrote that "America is neither dream nor reality. It is hyperreality. It is a hyperreality because it is a utopia which has behaved from the very beginning as though it were already achieved. Everything here is real and pragmatic, and yet it is all the stuff of dreams too."[15] The fiction of America that still rules the world. The fantasy of the great America that elected Trump—the president who, from its emblematic desert city of casino capitalism, a neon spectacle, reveals the excess and impotence of an American Dream attempting to escape its history of racist violence, which was also a revolutionary experiment in thought, technology, and the dream of a just society.

Across from Creech Air Force Base is Indian Springs, a small town of about a thousand inhabitants, 45 miles north of Las Vegas on Highway 95. Native Americans settled there for the water. During the early days of the twentieth century, Indian Springs was a railroad station between Tonopah and Las Vegas and, following the attack on Pearl Harbor, a training camp for the Army Air Force. After World War II, the Indian Springs Air Force was reactivated for aircraft research and the development of new weapons systems, including nuclear arms testing. Nearby is the Nevada Test Site where, since 1951, 105 nuclear bombs aboveground and 828 underground have been detonated. But Indian Springs would also be known for something quite different from the latest military technologies—extreme fantasy associated with UFOs. By the 1990s a new generation of drones was being developed in Area 51. Unmanned craft, without windows, cockpits, or the need to protect a pilot, took on "otherworldly" forms, including the shapes of flying saucers. Indeed, the drone industry evolved in close association with science fiction. The first official squadron of drones, soon to be deployed to the 1992-1995 Bosnia war, took shape at Indian Springs, the same town where UFO lore has it that Bob Lazar[16] was debriefed by extraterrestrials. In short, the initial

---

15   Baudrillard, *Simulacra*, 28.
16   Bob Lazar became well known for his claims that he reverse-engineered UFO technology and that the government possessed documents of extraterrestrial visits to the world for thousands of years. He brought the existence of Area 51, regularly

secret drones operated from Area 51 were at once drones and UFOs, surveillance tools and props for fantasy. Bergon's novel will bring to this same desert land a different type of fantasy—the monastic commitment to redeeming the world from sin and preventing the apocalypse.

"Dreamland [is] the critical core of the bomb,"[17] wrote Phil Patton. Dreamland or Area 51 is a world grounded in secrecy and "about mystery engendering fantasy."[18] But crucially, flying saucers "marched along in neat parallel to McCarthyism and the Red Scare."[19] Fantasy is a coin with two sides: images of the paradisiacal extraterrestrial world on the one side; images of fear and terror on the opposite side.

The military and the CIA always knew that the Cold War would mostly have to be fought at the level of the imagination and that a sophisticated system such as the U-2 plane was as much a psychological weapon as a reconnaissance tool. Just as there is a direct link between Area 51 and UFOs, there is also between Dreamland and Las Vegas—and between Las Vegas and Hollywood. Area 51's *Dreamland* is not only close to Las Vegas, "the city that never sleeps," but it is at the city's very core—its own *American Dream*, fed by the two-faced fantasies of extraterrestrial life and apocalyptic doom, erotic frenzy and suicidal fate. As for Hollywood, during the romantic period in the history of Las Vegas, Howard Hughes set aviation records and created an alliance between Hollywood and aerospace—that is, "Vegas was L.A. distillate, a step further into fantasy than even Hollywood would go."[20]

The president most closely connected to the Hollywood of Las Vegas and Area 51 was Ronald Reagan, the proponent of "Star Wars," a science fiction strategy engineered in Area 51. Like most other presidents in the modern era, Reagan cultivated and was beholden to Las Vegas money and influence. His belief in wonder weapons "was deeply rooted in his Hollywood past."[21] President Trump has promised to reinvent American missile defenses, a vision reminiscent of Reagan's Star Wars.

There are cultural and imaginary continuities between the Cold War and the War on Terror. In Joseph Masco's words, the " 'new' counterterror state in 2001 was actually a repetition, modeled in language and tone on the

---

visited by aliens according to him, to the attention of the general public.
17 Phil Patton, *Dreamland: Travels Inside the Secret World of Aroswell and Area 51* (New York: Villard, 1998), 56.
18 Ibid., 6.
19 Ibid., 97.
20 Ibid., 247.
21 Ibid., 209-210.

launch of the national security state in 1947."[22] From the beginning, the security state knew the power of fantasy, not only as a peril to be exploited by the enemy by provoking mass hysteria à la Orson Welles with his CBS radio broadcast of H. G. Wells's *The War of the Worlds*, which made many listeners believe that the earth was being attacked by Martians, but also as a fear-generating asset for controlling a docile citizenship. If "after the bombings of Hiroshima and Nagasaki [the Cold War] was fought incessantly at the level of imagination,"[23] so it is in the current War on Terror. Just as testing the atomic bomb in Nevada's desert became "the national fetish"[24] during the Cold War, weaponized drones in the same place currently involve a similar fetishistic goal.

From the Novel to an Ethnography of Resistance

It is in this desert America that Bergon places Abbot Arrizabalaga, the monk committed to the spiritual redemption of the world while living next to a nuclear test site where the destruction of mankind is being plotted by the greatest military power ever. I read Bergon's novel—with its central struggle between apocalypse and transfiguration—as I was doing my ethnography of drone warfare at Creech Air Base, 20 miles south of the test site. I was struck by the closeness of his literary fiction to what I was finding in the Nevada desert.

Bergon writes about his Abbot Arrizabalaga that "[f]or years activists had been pressing him to join the Franciscans in their protests at the Nevada Nuclear Test Site."[25] The leader of those Franciscans in the real Nevada of resistance to the NTS was Louie Vitale, a man Bergon knew about. I met Vitale in a nursing home in Oakland in the summer of 2017. He was born in Southern California in 1932. After graduating from college, he joined the U.S. Air Force and was at Nellis in 1957 when the first pacifist demonstrations against Operation Plumbbob atomic tests were taking place. A traumatic event would shake him and change the trajectory of his life: during a routine mission, he was ordered to shoot down an approaching

---

22 Joseph Masco, *The Theater of Operations: National Security Affect from the Cold War to the War on Terror* (Durham, NC: Duke University Press), 5.

23 Ibid., 16.

24 Joseph Masco, *Nuclear Borderlands: The Manhattan Project in Post-Cold War New Mexico* (2006; Princeton, NJ: Princeton University Press, 2006), 17.

25 *Temptations*, 24.

aircraft thought to be a Soviet military jet crossing into U.S. airspace. Three times the order was reiterated. At the last moment the crew decided to make a visual inspection and found that it was a commercial airliner, thus avoiding tragedy. This led to Vitale's decision to become a Franciscan. Vitale's prominent role among the Franciscans and his lifelong practice of "desert spirituality" would make him a pivotal figure in the resistance against the Nevada Test Site. Vitale has been arrested dozens of times. Among Vitale's most powerful experiences were his journeys to prisons where he found, he says, both irredeemable woundedness and sacredness.

In 1982, the 800th anniversary of St. Francis, Vitale led his community in organizing during Lent a radically new form of liturgy they named "The Lenten Desert Experience": "a series of nonviolent vigils over 40 days in the Nevada Test Site culminating in a civil disobedience action in which several dozens of us were arrested at the gates of the facility on Good Friday—and a joyful welcoming of the resurrection at the test site on Easter morning."[26] These actions were taking place in the context of Ronald Reagan's new administration's significant increase in nuclear weapons.

There is no complacency in Vitale's desert spirituality leading to a frontal denunciation of American militarism. "Many of us are alarmed, fearful, desperate, even angry," writes Vitale. "We worry for our children. We sense that our spirituality is inadequate to the challenges of our time. We need a new vision, or is it an old one?"[27] Religion for these men and women is anything but pious consolation; it has traumatized them and forced upon them a life of illegal actions and years in jail.

These Lenten days led to the formation of the Franciscan-based Nevada Desert Experience or NDE in Las Vegas. This organization integrates religious ritual and political action at the gates of the NTS—a combination of witnessing and militancy giving form to a new type of *desert spirituality* that incorporates antinuclear asceticism in a post-Hiroshima world, nonviolent practices that respect the opponent's views, and a modern adaptation of pilgrimage that journeys to the Nevada Test Site and to Creech as the symbolic centers of martial America.[28] Had Bergon's St. Ed Arrizabalaga known about NDE, he'd surely belong to it. As practiced by Vitale, the struggle against nuclear arms should not take the form of a conventional

---

26 Louie Vitale OFM, *Love Is What Matters: Writings on Peace and Nonviolence,* ed. Ken Butigan (Corvallis, OR: Pace e Bene Press, 2015), 15.
27 Ibid., 37.
28 See Ken Butigan, *Pilgrimage Through a Burning World: Spiritual Practice and Nonviolent Protest at the Nevada Test Site* (New York: State University of New York Press, 2003), xi-xii.

bipolar narrative of us versus them—in his view we all are responsible for what goes on at the Nevada Test Site, and we all belong to the same side. One of the Franciscan nuns who joined Vitale was Rosemary Lynch; she asked for an interview with General Mahlon Gates, the director of the Nevada Test Site at the time to ask him permission to erect a cross by the NTS's gate. They talked for an hour and a half and prayed together; later they appeared together on a Las Vegas television show. Shortly afterwards Gates resigned from his post.

Perhaps inspired by Rosemary Lynch, Bergon's Abbot Arrizabalaga also took part on a talk show in Las Vegas. On his way back to the hermitage he noticed that he was approaching Mercury, the town near the entrance to the Nuclear Test Site, a location he had seen on TV with images of protesters arrested and handcuffed, its topography evoking comparisons with Dachau. For Arrizabalaga, much as for the radicalized Franciscan men and women of the resistance I've met, the Nevada Test Site represents a holy site of apocalyptic dimension. This is the Desert of the Real where the ultimate battle between life and death is staged. For the Franciscans Vitale and Lynch, the Cross is the symbol central to their religious experience, the one they erected on Good Friday of 1982 at the test site with General Gates's permission. They began the tradition of practicing the "Stations of the Cross" that memorializes Christ's last hours. When I was a seminarian in my youth, the *via crucis* was a daily staple of my religious experience; forty years later I found myself doing the "Way of the Cross" on Good Friday of 2017. I wasn't sure whether I should attend as an ethnographer or as a participant. I asked Julia, my mentor at the Las Vegas Catholic Worker, whether I could take notes; she said no.

Bergon's novel also brings forth Shoshone shamans and Shoshone women fighting twenty-year battles with the government over their rights to graze cattle on their lands.[29] It is inside Shoshone Mountain that the government planned to place the nuclear waste dump. I met one of those shamans, Johnnie Bobb, the morning after Donald Trump won the presidency, when a dozen of us gathered in the predawn darkness around a ceremonial fire across from Creech Air Base in the Nevada desert. Smoke from burning cottonwood and cedar rose in the air as shoulder to shoulder, facing the fire, we stepped first in one direction, then the other, circling to the rhythm of Shoshone Chief Johnnie Bobb's chanting and drum. We were there to protest drone killing, prepared to be arrested at

---

29   *Temptations*, 81-82.

Creech for doing so. Johnnie gave each of us a cedar twig to throw into the fire as we spoke our thoughts.

The protests organized by the NDE gathered momentum year after year.[30] In 1985, 400 people participated at the Lenten Desert Experience and 28 were arrested. During the Hiroshima and Nagasaki anniversaries of the same year, 500 people participated and 121 were arrested. From May 31 to June 2, 1986, 1,200 people rallied in front of the NTS. On May 5, 1987, two Catholic bishops joined 96 others to be arrested. On May 10, various pacifist groups organized a Mother's Day Action which brought together 3,000 people and 790 people were arrested, bringing the issue to the attention of the national press. A high point was the march of May 8-16, 1988, in which 8,000 people participated with 2,065 arrests. On April 8-15, 1989, 1,800 people were arrested. In June 1991 over 400 women and men came from over 131 religious communities. After the collapse of the Soviet Union and under the relentless opposition of an international movement demanding an end to nuclear testing, President George H. W. Bush announced a moratorium in 1992. The Comprehensive Test Ban Treaty was signed by over 150 countries in 1996 (but is still unratified by the U.S.). The United States has continued designing and testing weapons at laboratories such as the Livermore National Laboratory and conducting what it terms "subcritical" explosive tests at the NTS. In February 2019, the Trump Administration withdrew from the landmark Intermediate-Range Nuclear Forces Treaty with Russia, signed by Reagan and Mikhail Gorbachev in 1987.

Kenotic Nothingness

When the novice Brother S tells Abbot Arrizabalaga that he expects "spiritual fulfillment" in the hermitage, he gets this reply from the abbot: "Forget it. I told you to expect nothing. A monk's purpose is not to find things; it is . . . to seek things. When will you realize who you really are?"[31] But this idea of nothingness is developed by Arrizabalaga most forcefully during the TV talk show he takes part in Las Vegas, hosted by Nathan Spock. As the host introduces him as a man who promises spiritual salvation, the abbot cuts him off:

---

30   These numbers are taken from Butigan, *Pilgrimage*, 73-75.
31   *Temptations*, 9.

"Wait a minute. I promise nothing."

"Nothing?"

"Nothing," he said.

"Not salvation?"

"No, not salvation."

"Not even happiness?"

"Especially not happiness."

"Peace?"

"No."

"Tranquility?"

"No."

"Transcendence?"

"No."

"What then?"

"Nothing."

"But you must offer something."

"No, those who come to the hermitage offer themselves."

"But to what end?"

"No end. They came for the means, not the end, to achieve nothing, to become nothing."[32]

Host Nathan Spock voices the question every listener must have been thinking: "Lunatic or saint? That's the question some people ask about Brother Edward Arrizabalaga, founder and leader of the Hermitage of Solitude in the Desert."[33]

In the tradition of Christian spirituality, since the fourth century the desert had represented *kenotic nothingness*, divinity's "emptying." A militant priest I met in Bilbao, Javi Vitoria, showed me what *kenosis* meant; he wrote about God's "impotence in the world" and about how "God's *kenosis* on the

32   Ibid., 19.
33   Ibid., 20.

cross leads to an authentic revolution in the image we have of God," leading to a Jewish mystical theme: "the one of God's *self-limitation* to give space to the existence and autonomy of the world."[34] Javi had earlier asked: "Why Gernika? Why Auschwitz? Why Hiroshima?" to then add: "This unending series of questions appears to postulate a declaration of the bankruptcy of faith in God and a complete discredit of the Augustinian name for God: 'I am your salvation.' "[35] But theology and mystical experience were not what really mattered to these men electrified by the spiritual, as it didn't to Bergon's Arrizabalaga, who felt the ground quiver from the Yucca Flat explosion of 150 kilotons, and who "sensed the glow in the sand and the hum in his skeleton as he drew closer to Shoshone Mountain and its fiery bowels of nuclear waste."[36] Political activism was the urgent thing to stop the nuclear madness. This is also the mission Bergon personally embodied when he got involved for years in the antinuclear movement.

One of the references in Bergon's novel is to the influential Trappist monk Thomas Merton. Louie Vitale also quoted him while jailed at Nellis AFB Federal Prison near Las Vegas: "Long ago, Thomas Merton called the desert 'a sacred place,' the proverbial Holy Ground of indigenous peoples, hermits, mystics, and pilgrims. We have turned the desert of Southern Nevada into the site of nuclear bombs and casinos. The work of the Nevada Desert Experience has been to reclaim the land as Holy Ground and end the evil of preparations for nuclear holocaust."[37] The desert wilderness was where John the Baptist lived and where Christ had been tempted. But earlier in the Scriptures the Exodus from Egypt marked the paradigmatic Passover experience—the forty years' journey through the desert before reaching the Promised Land.

Bergon's novel also mentions Ignatius of Loyola, "that old Basque soldier and founder of the Jesuits . . . whose spiritual exercises still transformed California boys into spiritual warriors."[38] Brother S met Jesuits in high school when he was fighting his lustful dreams.[39] In the resistance to drones and nuclear testing in Nevada, one finds the presence of the Jesuits, followers of Pedro Arrupe, who revolutionized the company of Jesus during the 1960s. Daniel Berrigan was a prominent example. In 1968 during the Vietnam War, the Berrigan brothers and seven other activists burned draft

---

34   F. Javier Vitoria, *El Dios cristiano* (Bilbao: Universidad de Deusto, 2008), 63, 65.
35   Ibid., 25.
36   *Temptations*, 292.
37   Vitale, *Love*, 52.
38   *Temptations*, 42.
39   Ibid., 152-53.

files with home-made napalm at Catonsville. Daniel Berrigan wrote then about "the Pentecostal fire of Catonsville."[40] As Berrigan said in his trial with the Catonsville nine, "one could not indefinitely obey the law" because "the bombings [of Vietnam] were a massive crime against humanity."[41]

The Death of Time

Abbot Ed Arrizabalaga was long working on a book entitled *The Death of Time*, which is also the title of chapter 5 in Bergon's novel, a book that began with the image of a photograph: the clock that stopped in Hiroshima at 8:16 a.m. on August 6, 1945. That image in Bergon's novel was also the anchor of Pedro Arrupe's existential experience, one he had personally witnessed in Hiroshima and that was present throughout his life. Arrupe wrote: "that clock, silent and immobile, has been for me a symbol. . . . Hiroshima has no relation to time: it belongs to eternity."[42]

Hiroshima marked for Arrupe and for Bergon's Arrizabalaga the end of time. *Time* is of course the difference between mythical and factual narratives, science fiction and actual reality.

There is no requirement of real time in fantasy or fiction. Nuclear deterrence and counterterrorism have a peculiar relation to time because threats and preemption, their basic aspects, are largely based on *future* events that give rise to a culture founded on the inevitability of waiting. Actual historical temporality becomes subservient to the feared future. If there are no terrorism attacks, the counterterrorist claims success in preventing them; but if the attack does occur, then the counterterrorist can say "I told you so" and argue that he was right in his predictions. Terrorism foretold becomes impervious to historical error and turns into prophecy fulfilled—a time warp at the heart of counterterrorist mythology, a self-fulfilling prophecy.

Robotic technology exacerbates the pressures on an axis of time. Robots react with such speed that the decision cycle gets reduced from minutes to microseconds. The apocalyptic scenario increasingly predicted is one in which, "[a]s the loop gets shorter and shorter, there won't be

---

40 Daniel Berrigan, *Essential Writings*, ed. John Dear (New York: Orbis, 2009), 123.
41 Ibid., 124, 133.
42 Arrupe qtd. in Gianna La Bella, *Pedro Arrupe, General de la Compañía de Jesús: Nuevas aportaciones a su biografía* (Bilbao: Mensajero, 2007),18.

any time in it for humans."[43] It is no longer the perversion of the axis of time in waiting for terror, but the very elimination of human time—the perfect fantasy by which not only will humans not have to fight and die but, by reducing time to the category of a technicality, they will not have to make the tough decisions nor carry the burden of their consequences. The "human baggage" will be sidelined to avoid faulty senses such as human eyes. "Pinpointed" is one of the magical words for robots firing missiles from far away—accompanied with the image of hitting the needle in a haystack.[44] A crucial issue in the application of robots for military use is robotic *autonomy*, prompting the question: who will make the final combat decisions, humans or robots? Although the initial assumption is that humans will delegate tasks to robots that will then need human permission for final decisions to act, "the problem is that it may not prove workable in reality."[45]

Berrigan, in the tradition of Loyola's new "seeing" after his conversion experience, wrote of a "second sight" by which he could "see washed ashore the last hour of the world, the murdered clock of Hiroshima."[46] But this new sight was not without consequences, for, as he stated in his poem "Prophecy": "The way I see the world is strictly illegal / To wit, through my eyes / Is illegal, yes . . . This is not permitted / that I look on the world / and worse, insist that I see / what I see/—a conundrum, a fury, a burning bush."[47] It was at the Nevada Test Site that the Jesuit Steve Kelly told me about Arrupe's visit to Berrigan in Danbury prison. Arrupe, the Bilbaino General of the Jesuits overcome by the technological and religious horror of Hiroshima, visited Berrigan, the American Jesuit repeatedly arrested for his opposition to nuclear weapons. Berrigan had taken advantage of the floodgates opened by Arrupe towards a theology of the poor and the oppressed and was following Arrupe's antinuclear stance. Just months before our meeting at the test site, Kelly, a participant himself in Plowshares actions and a veteran of years in federal prison, had spoken at the funeral of his long-time friend Berrigan. Berrigan's life experience, Kelly said, had been a "total commitment, not a partial desire," nourished by the "sacrament of resistance." Kelly also brought

---

43　An army colonel quoted in Peter Singer, *Wired for War: The Robotics Revolution and Conflict in the 21st Century* (New York: Penguin Books, 2009), 64.
44　The reality might be something different as we know from former drone pilots' testimonies in *National Bird*.
45　Singer, *Wired for War*, 126.
46　Berrigan, *Writings*, 28.
47　Ibid., 136-137.

to my attention the Jesuits murdered in El Salvador, whom Berrigan had befriended, as had the Jesuits followers of Arrupe I had met in Bilbao.

Conclusion: God Is an Explosion

In my sanctity-seeking youth, I lived in a convent for several years, and as I read this novel, I felt Frank knew too much about monks, their temptations, and in general about sanctity as the refusal of the world. His intimate knowledge of my former life piqued me enough that I decided to call him up and ask bluntly, *Have you been a monk yourself like I was?* Frank is a writer, and that in itself is monastic life enough, and fiction is more than sufficient knowledge for him. But if Frank got so carried away by monks and their love lives, something similar happened to me while writing my ethnography of drone warfare at Creech Air Base—it led me to relive my former monastic years at the Las Vegas Catholic Worker. You might think that the last thing you want to go to Las Vegas for is to become a monk—unless you are of course a writer like Frank in the process of inventing his desert hermitage or an ethnographer like me searching once again for the American soul in its military Dreamland. When I joined the anti-drone protesters at Creech, I noticed that some of the protesters at the makeshift Camp Justice wore Dorothy Day T-shirts. Day was the founder of the Catholic Worker movement whose Las Vegas branch fed the protesters during Shut-Down Creech Week. The more I came to know the protesters, the more I realized how much she mattered to them. I had met Dorothy Day by chance in October 1975 en route to Canada where I was going to study anthropology. When I stopped to visit a friend living on the Catholic Workers' farm in Tivoli, New York, Day, a tall and beautiful woman in her seventies, with a strong look her daughter Tamar described as "intense" and "devastating,"[48] lived there. In our brief encounter she gave me a gift—a Bible. Day's Catholic religiosity was conservative but rooted in a radical commitment to social and political action. Her intensity, combined with her comforting closeness, made my memory of her, like the Bible she gave me, a treasure. That's how chance works on you. When I told the Creech anti-drone protesters how I had met her and how "I wouldn't mind being a Catholic again in Dorothy's company," I felt their immediate warmth and acceptance. That's how, on

---

48   Quoted in Kate Hennessy, *Dorothy Day: The World Will Be Saved by Beauty* (New York: Scribner, 2017), 343.

Sunday October 9, 2016, I came to join 150 Catholic Worker members gathered 300 feet away from the Nevada Nuclear Test Site's entrance gate, sitting in a semicircle on makeshift pews to celebrate Mass officiated by Steve Kelly. A brass band played the African American spiritual "Down by the Riverside" as we walked through the desert surrounded by sagebrush and under a heavy sun. The celebration of Mass was not for us a banal gesture; it was a symbolic act to show who we were—either as Catholics, as Jews, or as atheists. But beyond symbolism we were most aware that we were in the desert of the Real—in the battle between reality and fiction, life and death.

I joined the Las Vegas Catholic Worker for three months. I would get up at 5:00 a.m. to a strong smell of chili peppers, tomato sauce, onion, garlic, celery, and carrots mixed with chicken or rice or beans and would help stirring the four large stewpots on the fire. At 6:00 we prayed. And by 6:25 we left the house, the food carefully placed in the caravan, moving slowly to the vacant lot a mile away to face five or six parallel lines of a couple of hundred homeless, while the morning sun was rising into the red Las Vegas sky. As they approached silently one by one with their paper plates in hand, I didn't dare look at their faces, I could barely say good morning. In 30 to 40 minutes, we were done, and we'd return to the house where I helped with the kitchen and the garden during the day. I was back in the convent, an atheist but still praying, unable to give up my adolescent desire for sanctity. I like to think that, with Frank's permission, Abbot Arrizabalaga would have accepted me into his Hermitage of Solitude in the Desert.

If Bergon brings the reader to face the axiomatic choice between the two clouds and the two types of transfigurations, in my ethnography of drone warfare I was confronted with something I labeled "the Westmoreland alternative"—that is, the choice between William Westmoreland, "the general who lost Vietnam,"[49] and Cian Westmoreland, the young drone operator introducing himself to us in Las Vegas as a war criminal who had helped kill 357 civilians. Both men were from the same extended family with lives defined by service to their country. But the two combatants couldn't have been be more fundamentally opposed in their thinking and subjective response to their actions and responsibilities, as well as how they experienced or denied the traumas that connected them.

---

49   See Lewis Sorley, *Westmoreland: The General Who Lost Vietnam* (Boston: Mariner Books, 2012).

Having experienced the underground nuclear explosions in the nearby desert, Bergon's St. Ed Arrizabalaga found himself explaining to his bishop the Yiddish proverb, "God is an explosion, not an uncle."[50] The proverb is not as absurd as it initially seems if you consider that many people think of God as a benevolent uncle ready to help you each time you ask for some favor. In the tradition of explosive Christianity once I heard Julia, the head of the Las Vegas Catholic Workers, give a talk in which she quoted Dorothy Day: "an experience of the living God is a terrible thing." Day often quoted Dostoevsky's Father Zossima: "Love in practice is a harsh and dreadful thing compared with love in dreams."[51] For Day the systematic planning for the nuclear holocaust falls into a murderous purpose, a crime that is committed *now* under the name of deterrence. There is no better insight into the spirituality of Day and her followers protesting at the NTS and Creech than Dostoevsky's paradoxical theodicy, summed up thus by one of Day's favorite thinkers, Nikolai Berdyaev: "The existence of evil is a proof of the existence of God. If the world consisted wholly and uniquely of goodness and righteousness there would be no need for God, for the world itself would be god. God is, because evil is. And that means that God is because freedom is."[52] For the men and women I found protesting in the Nevada desert, the killings of civilians by drones and the nuclear buildup for the end of humanity—the epitome of Evil calling for a redeeming God—make that place at once apocalyptic and sacred.

Bergon's novel is a sustained study of the true nature of love and sexuality; the life of his celibate monks with their "temptations" and falls provides Bergon ample opportunity to meditate on love. Early in the novel, as St. Ed takes part in the Las Vegas talk show, we see him on the defensive arguing that their monastic life is not about turning back time but living in time, not about escaping life's realities but finding them. "Isn't it true that you've renounced sex," the host asks, not surprisingly, this being Las Vegas. "We're celibate," replies Arrizabalaga, who had been married before becoming a monk, "I wouldn't say we have renounced sex."[53] This is a hermitage in the middle of nowhere and after fifteen years of prayer and proselytizing Arrizabalaga had succeeded in achieving only one vocation, Brother S. And it was far from sure that he would turn the novice into a true monk. The temptations were many. Most prominently

50 *Temptations*, 187.
51 Dorothy Day, *Selected Writings*, ed. Robert Ellsberg (Maryknoll, NY: Orbis Books, 1983), 264.
52 Nicholas Berdyaev, *Dostoevsky* (New York: Meridian Books, 1957), 87.
53 *Temptations*, 22.

there was one source of disquiet for Brother S—Amy, a young woman he found injured on the road after a truck accident while he was walking in the desert with his dogs on a day in which the abbot St. Ed was in Las Vegas. He brought her to the hermitage, obliged to take care of injuries and her broken truck. A friendship developed that would sorely test and ultimately ruin his vow of celibacy; furthermore, St. Ed himself, after a peyote joint ceremony with the Shoshone shamans, falls in love with Amy. "Why can't people be both monks and lovers?" Amy asks Brother S, who replies "St. Ed says there's no love so intense, so all-consuming, as celibate love."[54] Monks falling for Amy could only signal shipwreck from the traditional monastic perspective—unless you follow Rimbaud's maxim that "love is to be reinvented,"[55] which is what Arrizabalaga did. You could hear him preaching that "Life is not a battle between the spirit and the flesh . . . It's un-Christian to think so. Life is a battle between love and selfishness . . . We are to be passionate; we're to be erotic. Eros, when refined, explodes into unselfish love." What mattered for Arrizabalaga was the choice between the mushroom cloud or the Cloud of the Unknowing.

In short, Bergon found decades ago the best solution possible to the endemic problem of the Catholic Church's sexual scandals—turn the temptress Amy into Mother Amy, the abbess of Arrizabalaga's revolutionary order. This appears to be a solution inspired by Mari of Anboto, the queen of Basque witches, as well as St. Bernard, the founder of the Cistercians who wrote about some mythical White Monks and about restoring a lost religion, one that Arrizabalaga traced to his "paleolithic precursors," for "[t]he White Monks became like pre-Arian Basques in Neolithic times, when their highest deity was a goddess and her consort was a snake."[56] You might think that, despite my insistence on the desert of the Real, there is in fact too much fiction in the lives of these desert monks and Las Vegas Catholic Workers. To this Bergon's Arrizabalaga would reply in self-defense: "Forget it. I promised nothing. God is not an uncle."

---

54   Ibid., 100-101.
55   Arthur Rimbaud, *Complete Works, Selected Letters*, ed. Wallace Fowlie (Chicago: University of Chicago Press, 1966), 281.
56   *Temptations*, 186.

WORKS CITED

Baudrillard, Jean. *Simulacra and Simulation*. Ann Arbor: University of Michigan Press, 1994.

———*America*. With an Introduction by Geoff Dyer. London: Verso, 2010.

Berdyaev, Nicholas. *Dostoevsky*. New York: Meridian Books, 1957.

Bergon, Frank. *The Temptations of St. Ed & Brother S*. Reno: University of Nevada Press, 1993.

Berrigan, Daniel. *Daniel Berrigan: Essential Writings*. Selected with an Introduction by John Dear. New York: Orbis Books, 2009.

Butigan, Ken. *Pilgrimage Through a Burning World: Spiritual Practice and Nonviolent Protest at the Nevada Test Site*. New York: State University of New York Press, 2003.

Corrigan, Maureen. *So We Read On: How the Great Gatsby Came to Be and Why It Endures*. New York: Little, Brown and Company, 2014.

Day, Dorothy. *Dorothy Day: Selected Writings*, edited and with an Introduction by Robert Ellsberg. Maryknoll, New York: Orbis Books, 1983.

Fitzgerald, F. Scott. *The Great Gatsby*. New York: Scribner, 1925.

La Bella, Gianni, ed. *Pedro Arrupe, General de la Compañía de Jesús: Nuevas aportaciones a su biografía*. Bilbao: Mensajero, 2007.

Hennessy, Kate. *Dorothy Day: The World Will Be Saved by Beauty*. New York: Scribner, 2017.

Masco, Joseph. *Nuclear Borderlands: The Manhattan Project in Post-Cold War New Mexico*. Princeton, NJ: Princeton University Press, 2006.

———. *The Theater of Operations: National Security Affect from the Cold War to the War on Terror*. Durham, NC: Duke University Press, 2014.

Patton, Phil. *Dreamland: Travels Inside the Secret World of Roswell and Area 51*. New York: Villard, 1998.

Rimbaud, Arthur. *Rimbaud: Complete Works, Selected Letters*. Edited with an Introduction by Wallace Fowlie. Chicago: University of Chicago Press, 1996.

Singer, Peter W. *Wired for War: The Robotics Revolution and Conflict in the 21st Century.* New York: Penguin Books, 2009.

Sorley, Lewis. *Westmoreland: The General Who Lost Vietnam.* Boston: Mariner Books, 2012.

Thompson, Hunter S. *Fear and Loathing in Las Vegas.* New York: Vintage Books, 1998.

Vitale, Louie OFM. *Love Is What Matters: Writings on Peace and Nonviolence.* Edited by Ken Butigan. Corvallis, OR: Pace e Bene Press, 2015.

Vitoria, F. Javier. *El Dios cristiano.* Bilbao: Universidad de Deusto, 2008.

Zizek, Slavoj. *Welcome to the Desert of the Real.* New York: The Wooster Press, 2001.

Zupancic, Alenca. *The Shortest Shadow: Nietzsche's Philosophy of the Two.* Cambridge: MIT Press, 2003.

Unheard Voices of Okie California

Zeese Papanikolas

Of course you have heard these voices. You might remember driving down the Central Valley before you could drop your own discs into the deck or open the lid of Pandora's music box, and, out of boredom or distraction, twisted the dial for the local radio AM stations. There they were, these voices with their country edge, giving the weather, the farm report, the local news, exhorting you to come to Jesus between twanging songs about heartbreak and hell raising. You might have faintly imagined, on that drive, that these voices had always been there, floating history-less as the clouds above the cottonwood trees and the crops. But in fact, they are the voices of a great twentieth-century migration, that of rural folk from Dust Bowl Arkansas and Oklahoma, Texas, New Mexico, Missouri, and other states, who set out in jalopies and trucks held together by bailing wire and desperation on the trek to California in the 1930s.

We heard their voices captured by John Steinbeck in a novel that will one day return to critical acclaim, called *The Grapes of Wrath*. Some of us, at least, have heard that Okie twang in the wry and angry songs Woody Guthrie sang about the exodus. But *The Grapes of Wrath* is on somebody's list of books you should reread someday, and Woody Guthrie lives on only through college radio stations or left-wing FM (if he ever did have much of an audience outside the left in the first place). There is a kind of vocal muting going on here that disconnects those voices of the past from the children and grandchildren of the Dust Bowl migration who still live among us.

After *The Grapes of Wrath*, there is a strange emptiness in California writing about these migrants and their progeny. They don't, after all, fit in with romantic conceptions of people of the soil, and they seem too stubborn and independent, too religious, too patriotic to be cast as a leftist proletariat. There are exceptions to this silence of course, Gerald Haslam's stories and essays and Roxanne Dunbar-Ortiz's evocation of an

Okie childhood and a California education, to name two.[1] So, though the voices are all around us, we don't hear them in the sense I'm talking about because in our minds they are cut off from their roots in history, drifting free on the airways, generic "country voices" that might have come from a rural American anywhere. If you don't know where the Californians among them come from, you're not hearing them.

From 1935 through 1940 there were over seven hundred thousand of these southwesterners in California. They made up 10% of the population of the state, and almost 20% of the population of the San Joaquin Valley.[2] The lives of these migrants as they traveled the road to California and in migrant camps and tar paper shacks at the edges of Central Valley towns, where they scratched together lives as crop pickers and farm workers, were unforgettably documented by Dorothea Lange and other Farm Security Administration photographers and newspaper archives that tell the stories of their struggles and the often hostile reception they got as they fled the parched fields of their homes and fought to enter the golden state of California.[3]

Before the First World War there had been a strong populist streak in the Southwest that had led to the largest Socialist Party membership in the United States. According to James N. Gregory's comprehensive book, *American Exodus*, Socialists claimed over a third of Oklahoma's poorer counties and were strong in Arkansas and Northern Texas.[4] In 1917, the Green Corn Rebellion, a brief armed rebellion of black and white tenant farmers and Muscogee Indians against the World War I draft, was put down by a posse of Oklahomans.[5] But with the coming of the war itself, the post-war red scare, and the revival of the Ku Klux Klan, radical affiliation in the Southwest died. Facing horrific conditions and exploitation in California, migrant workers from the Dust Bowl took part in the sporadic strikes, sometimes of considerable magnitude, that broke

---

1   See, for example, Roxanne Dunbar-Ortiz , *Red Dirt: Growing Up Okie* (1997; Norman: University of Oklahoma Press, 2006); Gerald Haslam, *Haslam's Valley* (Berkeley, CA: Heyday Books, 2005.)

2   James N. Gregory, *American Exodus: The Dust Bowl Migration and Okie Culture in California* (New York: Oxford University Press, 1989), 251.

3   Dorothea Lange and Paul Schuster Taylor, *An American Exodus* (1939; New Haven: Yale University Press, 1969). For Lange and other Farm Security Administration photographers, see Hank O'Neal, *A Vision Shared: A Classic Portrait of America and Its People, 1935 -1943* (New York, St. Martin's Press, 1976).

4   Gregory, *American Exodus*, 158.

5   *Oklahoma Green Corn Rebellion* is an excellent online archive of articles and contemporaneous newspaper accounts of the rebellion, which centered in Sasakwa, Oklahoma.http://grencorn.org/ (accessed January 20, 2019).

out in the cotton fields and stoop crop fields in the Central Valley.[6] The migrants were often vilified. One San Joaquin Valley doctor called them "shiftless trash who live like hogs." Another doctor was kinder; still, for him the Okies and Arkies were "a strange people—they don't seem to know anything. They can't read at all. There is nothing especially wicked about them—it's just the way they live . . . they are like a different race." The children of these migrants were isolated and shamed because of their accents, their poverty, their ways. One of them told his teacher "We ain't people we are sharecroppers."[7] "I hated being poor," another said, remembering those days. "I hated wearing pasteboard in my shoes and twine for shoestrings, and I hated wearing hand-me-downs. I remember as a little kid saying, 'Boy, when I get big I ain't never gonna be poor again.' "[8] That past hangs like a shadow around *Jesse's Ghost*.

In 1947 when migrants from the Southwest were still pouring into California to work in booming post-World War II industries, memories and stories of that first migration out of the Dust Bowl were still fresh, but far enough away so that the bitterness of those days could be converted into comic irony.

> Oh dear Okie, if you see Arkie
>
> Tell him Tex got a job for him out in Californy
> Pickin' up prunes, squeezin' oil out of olives . . .
>
>
> Tex's jobs go on . . .
>
>
> Rakin' up gold, playin' fiddle in the follies . . .
> Sellin' used cars, just a-waitin' for the suckers . . .
> Working in a bank, all he needs is some money . . .

---

6 Gregory, *American Exodus*, 155-157. See also Carey McWilliams, *Factories in the Field: The Story of Migratory Farm Labor in California* (1935; Berkeley: University of California Press, 2000), 312-314.

7 Ibid., 100-101, 132.

8 Country-western singer and composer Buck Owens (1929-2006), quoted in Gerald Haslam, with Alexandra Haslam Russell, and Richard Chon, *Workin' Man Blues: Country Music in California* (Berkeley, CA: Heyday Books, 1999), 208.

But there's one line in Doye O' Dell's song that goes beyond this satire and has a poignancy that is very much a part of *Jesse's Ghost*. It is about Tex's and Okie's and Arkie's children:

> Now he'll be lucky if he finds a place to live But there's orange juice fountains flowin' for those kids of his[9]

This is the sound of the often unvoiced hope of these migrants for their children, a hope that goes beyond survival and into a vision of a better life. As for these children themselves, what remained were memories of those early days. An Okie named Merle Haggard, who grew up in Oildale in a converted railroad boxcar, sang of such memories:

> A canvas-covered cabin in a crowded labor camp, stand out in this memory I revive.
>
> 'Cause my daddy raised a family there, with two hard- working hands,
>
> And tried to feed my mama's hungry eyes.

The children in Haggard's song were too young to realize what they would soon enough know, that "another class of people" put them "somewhere just below."[10] In 1958, about the time that Frank Bergon' s novel *Jesse's Ghost* begins, Merle Haggard was in San Quentin prison, serving time for robbery and picking out chords on a guitar.

Thus, one way of thinking about *Jesse's Ghost* is as a generational novel, part of a long tradition of American books that trace the struggles of the second generation of immigrant children with their parents' old-country past and the new world in which they set out to find a place. Because of their poverty, their cultural "otherness," the Okies of Bergon's novel really *are* immigrants in their own land, but by the time the book begins they have come to the Central Valley to stay. The first generation of migrants still

---

9   Doye O'Dell (1912-2001), "Dear Okie," recorded in Los Angeles in 1947. Exclusive 33x (EXC 1188-2).

10   Merle Haggard (1937-2016), "Hungry Eyes," Tree Publishing Co. Inc., 1969, 1971. For information on Buck Owens, Doye O'Dell, and Merle Haggard, see their entries in Haslam, *Workin' Man Blues*.

live in Little Oklahoma, eat Okie food, and have kept their southwestern accents and speech, but almost twenty years have passed since a Madera mob had attacked cotton pickers with pick handles and clubs and broken their strike.[11] Okie boys are no longer shabby and half-starved. They go to school with the local Latinos and African Americans and the sons and daughters of local ranchers, they wrestle and play high school football, and they don't much listen to country-western music. As for other American kids of their generation, the pounding rock and roll they hear at Bass Lake where they fight bikers and dance with the local girls and the treacly pop songs about teenage love are the soundtracks of their young lives, but if I'm not mistaken there is the same kind of sadness under their violence and their sexual conquests that you hear in those wailing country-western songs. There is as well the anger in them of some of those songs as they fight for recognition in the world into which they have been born.

Jesse's Ghost is the story of two of these Okie boys growing up in the San Joaquin Valley town of Madera in the 1950s and of a friendship that becomes more than the momentary alliance of a couple of kids from Little Oklahoma as they compete for the local girls, fight each other and others and enter the world of farm labor. It is also the story of how the conjunction of love and violence comes to inhabit the mind of one of these boys.

> The story of how I came to kill my best friend keeps pressing on my brain like a dream so bad I can feel it, but I can't remember it whole. In bed at night when I can't sleep—just about every night anymore— bits of my life buzz and clatter in my skull. "I will haunt you when I'm dead," my mother told me all the time when I was a kid, yet the person who haunts me now is the friend I loved more than my momma or my daddy or even my own brother. His name was Jesse Floyd.[12]

This is the voice of Sonny Childers, long out of prison, brooding about the murder of his best friend in an empty house. It is a voice that contains many other voices in the novel, the voices of Little Oklahoma, the voices of Dixieland, the home of Madera's African Americans, and of Mex Town where Hispanic migrants and perhaps even descendants of California's first European settlers live, and the voice of his friend Mitch Etcheverry

---

11   Gregory, *American Exodus*, 157.
12   Frank Bergon, *Jesse's Ghost* (Berkeley, CA: Heyday, 2011), 1.

who like him speaks the language of seventeen- and eighteen-year-old boys in the 1950s, raunchy and boastful, crude and aggressive. The jokes these friends—Sonny and Jesse Floyd and Mitch Etcheverry—tell, their fights, the crude pranks they play on each other, are the stuff of their bonds. Their jokes are both familiar to them and funny, too.

Driving an old truck in one of Mitch Etcheverry's father's fields, Sonny has trouble shifting gears. "I can't find the hole," he tells Mitch. "Put some hair around it," Mitch answers. "As I knew he would," Sonny continues. But Mitch also speaks another language, for he is not the son of a worker but of a successful rancher, goes to a private school outside San Jose, and will go on to college—it is Mitch who can quote the *Odyssey* in Greek and give a glimpse of a world beyond the Valley. There are too the voices of Father Dan, a Catholic priest, himself the son of a Coalinga oilfield worker; of Old Antiguo; of Cowboy Duane, an Okie turned cowboy whose voice sounds like a record on slow play; of Jesse Floyd as he recites one of his spur-of-the moment poems, the voices in the songs they listen to, of the girls they chase and sometimes catch—and who catch them.

It might seem a long way from the Central Valley in the 1950s to Stalin's Russia, but that great critic Mikhail Bakhtin provides an entry into what I think is one of the most significant sides of Bergon's book in his essay "Discourse in the Novel." For Bakhtin, *the* meaning of the novel was found in its voices; voices that carry within them a whole history, a whole sociology, classes and professions, generations and educations. It is out of the tension among these voices—constantly moving and changing discursive perspectives as they impinge upon each other in an open series of dialogues—that the novel is made.[13] Sonny's voice contains all of the voices of his youth, but also traces of the languages he has heard since: newer slang, newer phrases, even sometimes a hint of the stuff he gets out of the soap operas he watches while nursing a disability. His voice in the novel is an encyclopedia of Valley voices present and past. But mostly it is that of a boy from Madera's Little Oklahoma.

The link to the Okie past in the novel is Sonny's stepfather Dewey. Dewey is a great character. He drinks and he fights, and his Okie sense of honor has a hole in it when it comes to marital fidelity—"He'd fuck a woodpile if he thought there was a snake in it" Sonny says of him at

---

13   Mikhail Mikhailovich Bakhtin, "Discourse in the Novel," in M. M. Bakhtin, *The Dialogic Imagination: Four Essays*, ed. Michael Holquist, tr. Caryl Emerson and Michael Holquist (Austin: University of Texas Press, 1981).

one time.[14] Dewey almost beheads a man in a bar fight, and he beats his stepsons silly if they don't live up to the code he schools them in, a code that says drunk or sober you show up on the job, that says you never back down from a fight. A code that has a certain old-fashioned respect for the dignity of elders—"Yes, sir. No ma'am. Mr. or Mrs." Yet Dewey loves these children. Loved them enough to get them and their mother out of Oklahoma.

Okies like Sonny Childers and like Jesse Floyd—he was born in fact in Texas—carry that code with them, as they carry the violence of their families and the humiliating sting of the jeers of the children who didn't grow up on beans and cornbread or live in shacks in Little Oklahoma, or like Sonny, before his family moved to the Etcheverry farm, in a canvas tent with a rough plank floor. They knew that whatever they got in this world, whatever would take them out of the poverty of their parents, they would have to fight for. They fought the kids at school who taunted them, they fought their big brothers, they fought each other. "What Okie kid didn't fight?" Sonny says. "He fought to survive. He had to fight for everything he got. But he wanted something more."[15] What that more is—this is the great issue of the book.

Love and Violence

The bond between Sonny Childers and Jesse Floyd that is at the heart of this book is more than friendship. On Sonny's part, it is love. This story of the rivalry and love between brothers is very old, as old as the Mesopotamian hero Gilgamesh and his companion Enkidu, the wild man Gilgamesh fought and tamed. Older than another story that also ends with a hero mourning his companion-in-arms, one that Mitch Etcheverry knows well and that Jesse Floyd unknowingly parodies when he sends Sonny off to a dance in another town wearing his practice football jersey, for Achilles and Patroclus in Homer's *Iliad* were such friends, and Patroclus went to battle wearing Achilles's armor. Unlike Sonny, Patroclus was killed, while Sonny only ended up scratched to pieces by the girlfriends of one of Jesse's temporary conquests.[16] Sonny admires Jesse, he admires his courage and his fists—Sonny could beat Jesse in wrestling or boxing—but the kind

---

14   *Jesse's Ghost*, 52.
15   Ibid., 34.
16   Ibid., 27.

of fighting Jesse is a master at, the source of his reputation, has only one rule: to win, win with cunning, with feet, with fists, with trickery—any way. Sonny admires as well his friend's panache, his wit, his quickness with his words. (Jesse anticipates Muhammad Ali with his pre-fight spontaneous poems.) Jesse is great with the girls too, a dancer who invents something called the Hydro and can show his sheer strength by lifting a girl above his head as he moves across the floor. Sonny is always in Jesse's shadow, as he knows, yet it is a shadow that doesn't obscure him, it illuminates him. He is proud to be Jesse's friend, just as he was proud to hear kids at the dance in Merced taking him for Jesse when he walked in wearing the jersey with Jesse's number on it. But the other side of admiration is a kind of, unaddressed, unknown rage.

We see this early in the book when something happens that seems to have no context or motivation. Mitch Etcheverry, Jesse Floyd, and Sonny Childers are cruising Madera's main drag, Jesse driving, Sonny riding shotgun. Mitch and Jesse have been drinking cheap wine, but Sonny has only pretended to drink, waiting his chance. All at once he smashes Jesse hard under the ear. Jesse slams on the brakes, and the two boys go at it, but it is Mitch, as he tries to come between them, who ends up catching Jesse's fist as Sonny ducks.[17] It is the third time—but it will not be the last—that Sonny has tried to beat his best friend. These two powerful drives, love and violence, are so tightly braided in the book that only physical separation, or the ultimate separation of death, can untangle them.

The violence comes out of the past of these Okie kids and their families, but if the causes are there, they don't explain the sheer joy of victory in a fight. Sonny tries to explain it to Mitch. "Jesse just loved to fight," he says. "You can't ignore the pleasure of it. There's no better feeling than kicking the shit out of somebody."

There is something erotic in all of this. This joy, this release, is a cleansing affirmation of the bond between Sonny and Jesse, an affirmation of their relationship to each other that for a moment strips it of its ambiguities, strips it of envy and anger. Sonny tests himself against Jesse to know who he is, to affirm himself as an opponent worthy of his friend. But Sonny's wife—his second wife, Lynette—has heard this last moment of the conversation between Mitch and Sonny. Is there really no better pleasure than pounding another man into the ground? "None?" she asks. "None in the world?"[18]

---

17 Ibid., 6–7.
18 Ibid., 36.

Yet in this book of voices, there is, at its center, a curious silence: Jesse's. He speaks and he acts—with courage, generosity, or rage—but he is unknowable. We catch sight of him often, his smile that broke like sunshine—it is almost a Homeric epithet—his confidence that charms adults, charms the girls and the boys who admire him and would like to have so much as a nod from him. Fueled by the roiling anger inside him (and endless drinks of fortified milk), even Jesse's farts are heroic.[19] We hear him taunting his opponents with his improvised poems before pulverizing them under his fists and boots.[20] We hear him laying it on the girls: "The way *I* feel . . . makes *me* think . . . I *must* be . . . *in love.*"[21] He is a storyteller, and it is worth spending a moment on one of his tales, told for the entertainment of Sonny and a group of admiring boys about his new club, the 4 Cs or the Central California Crotch Cannibals. In the course of his explanation of the club, Jesse recounts why he broke up with a beautiful girl named Adelaide whom he had passed on to Sonny. "I had my head up there and found a necktie . . . and then somebody's sunglasses. This was too much for me, so I told her, 'Call Sonny.' " But he deftly pulls back, in order not to shame his friend, saying actually Sonny had gotten her away from him and after that he'd only "dipped his wick" about two more times. He is a prince who knows how to make a subject the butt of a joke, then raise him up again, but at the same time remind him that he is still the sovereign, still "number one rooster in the hen house."[22] Yet we know, and Sonny knows, that Jesse had refused to marry Adelaide when she thought she was pregnant, and that he had passed his friend on to her as some sort of consolation prize.

This then is the Jesse Floyd of the first part of the book, a golden youth, the pride of the dawn, as Federico García Lorca might have said, the hardpan kid, wrestling slabs of rock-hard earth into a truck, tirelessly swamping lugs of tomatoes with his powerful arms, a storyteller and lover, a fighter, a young Achilles singing to Patroclus in his tent, a hero who has all he desires by right of conquest.

Out of high school and on their own, the lives of Jesse, Mitch, and Sonny remain twined through the girls, now young women, to whom they are connected. Mitch goes off to college, Sonny continues his life as a worker, and Jesse Floyd is still fighting. When Jesse buys into a septic tank pumping business, he has the kind of angry drive that he showed in his

---

19   Ibid., 49.
20   Ibid., 9, 79.
21   Ibid., 27.
22   Ibid., 112.

battles, fighting with hands and feet and quickness of mind, anything to get an edge, to succeed. His brother has become a millionaire twice-over developing shopping centers. Jesse has already bought farmland. He is going to be unstoppable.[23]

By 1969, when Jesse's story drives to its violent conclusion, Merle Haggard had been out of prison ten years and was singing what became a kind of anti-hippie anthem during the Vietnam War, "Okie From Muskogee." Buck Owens, the Dust Bowl kid with pasteboard in his shoes who vowed never to be poor when he grew up, had settled in Bakersfield, had his own music publishing company and in two decades would be singing "Act Naturally" with Ringo Starr. Doye O' Dell, who gave us "Dear Okie," had acted in movies with Roy Rogers and Ronald Reagan; and Jesse Floyd was dead, killed by Sonny Childers, who had learned he was seeing his estranged first wife. Who was Jesse Floyd, after all? Like the country voices at the beginning of this essay, if we hear him, we don't know him. He is the absence that haunts this book and around which its action and its moral questioning revolve.

"He held his own, he kept his word, and he always got the girl," Mitch says in that long night of drinking that begins the book. "If he wasn't busting you in the face, he was fun to be with."

> "That's what made him a hero," Sonny answers.
> "He was a punk," Mitch says.
> "Jesse Floyd was no punk," Sonny answers.
> "He fucked you up good, Sonny. He didn't care about you. He crossed the line."[24]

In the course of the novel Sonny comes to know better than anyone the price of living in the reflected light of Jesse's charisma. "Your whole life is a lie," his estranged wife tells him on the night he killed Jesse and tried to kill her. Jesse puts in the final stab in a terrible final phone call. He says what Sonny has never been unable to admit: "You know you were always second choice."[25]

---

23   Ibid., 172.
24   Ibid., 22-23
25   Ibid., 184-185.

Language and Memory

One of Bergon's readers, the novelist John Vernon, speaks of the "informed nostalgia" of *Jesse's Ghost*. Nostalgia has a double meaning in this book. Sonny's nostalgia is for an irretrievable past, when, in his retrospective gaze, everything was whole, the fights, the girls, the work, and his friendship with Jesse. But nothing was whole. The fractures were there, but he didn't see them, and his nostalgia is for a life that ended abruptly and brutally with his murder of his best friend. Out on disability from a good job, in constant pain from the beatings of a life of work and fighting, abandoned to his own despair by a woman who has loved him (and who still turns heads when they walk into a restaurant), nothing can repair the hole in his past. Yet beneath that sense of a loss that can't be made up for by steady work, a house in the foothills, a good woman, or even hard-won understanding, there is something else.

At one point in the novel, Mitch and Sonny are drinking beer and Snap-E-Tom after a brutal day of work. They have been dumped by their girlfriends, are busted by hangovers and smeared with mud and goose shit, and are waiting to be jumped by three tough thugs. "Still," Mitch said, "someday we're probably going to look back on this as the best time of our life."[26] This anticipatory nostalgia is informed by its realism. Yet, as this passage shows, it is a realism shot through with pathos—pathos and a certain tenderness. The tenderness you can hear in Merle Haggard's best songs. The tenderness that is at the core of this book and that will prepare Sonny for redemption.

The Land

There is one final voice in this book that is important, a voice that can only speak through Sonny: the voice of nature. I don't mean to say that nature is a mystique in this novel, for nature is as hard and unforgiving here as in any book you can name, and the life on the land is one of endless work as the seasons turn, bringing the earth to fruition: plowing, planting, vee-ing out ditches, setting siphon pipes, moving irrigation lines, flagging the cropduster planes in the predawn darkness. It is water, water from the pumps of the Etcheverry fields whining day and night, spewing out the

---

26   Ibid., 76.

precious fluid from the deep, chilly ground, "that made the land hum."[27] The water of each well had its own taste, and Sonny remembers how he and Jesse and Mitch all had their favorites. That cold, pure water they drank straight from the pumps that flowed into the fields is an emblem of a pastoral innocence.

"After I again changed my water in the alfalfa field at around one in the morning," Sonny recalls,

> I watched the moon come up over the Sierras—a mountain range I couldn't see but knew to be there because of how the moon popped into view higher than the valley horizon. It was a half-moon, almost three-quarters, silvery but less pale than in early summer. Moonlight brightened the ditch water creeping over the ground like slow-moving mercury as it twisted around the alfalfa stalks, giving the air a sweet, musty smell. I liked irrigating at night when it was quiet and peaceful this way . . . [28]

This is not nostalgia, we come to realize, but elegy.

At the end of the book, Sonny imagines the Valley as the first Europeans might have seen it, with the sky thick with clouds of geese and ducks, and elk and even grizzlies roaming in the wild grass.[29] It is a California Eden. But Sonny also remembers winter rains that flooded the Etcheverry ranch, burying trucks and Caterpillar tractors and marooning a group of migrant workers in their cabins. The land itself has kept a record of the droughts that have periodically desiccated its soil, turning pieces of land into the obdurate hardpan crust that must be ripped away by tractors so that fields can be renewed.[30] But the very large-scale, industrial agriculture that made the Great Central Valley an incredible source of abundance could be its undoing. Hundreds of years of pumping for irrigation have drawn down the deep underground aquifers that have existed since the retreat of the glaciers that carved the valley, and they can never be fully replenished. The water, too, we know, is slowly being poisoned by the same chemicals that filled the tanks of the cropdusters and that poisoned Mitch's father and left Sonny covered in yellow sulphur. So the lyricism

---

27   Ibid., 131.
28   Ibid., 125.
29   Ibid., 197.
30   Ibid., 14, 160-161.

of Sonny's response to this land that he works, to its life-giving water, a lyricism earned by backbreaking labor, has a certain poignancy, for a reader who knows present-day California knows that the water under the fields of alfalfa and cotton is not inexhaustible, that the same kind of disaster that ripped the topsoil from Dust Bowl farms in Arkansas and Oklahoma and the Texas panhandle and blew it away may be the future of the Great Central Valley.[31]

Late in the book, Mitch and Sonny drive back to the ranch Mitch's father owned, where they both worked as kids, the ranch that once hummed with life, with the sounds of the irrigation pumps and the farm machinery, with the scrape of Old Antigua's rake endlessly sweeping under the trees that shaded the ranch house, with the voices of the cowboys joking in the feedlot they leased. All this is gone, the ranch has been sold, its buildings torn down, its winding stream straightened. It is a reversal of the myth of nature as healing mother. Here the land itself is sick. Everything is gone.

The nostalgia for this past could turn into a sickness, a bitter disease, unless something can be found in it that can bring it into the realm of grace—for ultimately, though not in any conventional sense, this is a book about grace. It is grace that will reconcile the voices in this book, that will make sense of what can't be made sense of in any other way. There is a character in the novel, one might call him a minor character, but I think he is in fact central to understanding this project of redemption: Nellie, the dwarfish nephew of Old Antiguo, who spends his days raking. Nellie lives in a shack on the ranch and spends his time drinking and watching primitive porn movies—and searching the heavens with a telescope through which, for the first time, Sonny sees the rings of Saturn. For there is a world beyond the small patch of ground that Sonny knows—a universe, in fact. It is Nellie who has told Sonny that the land is sinking because the Valley farms are sucking up its hidden water. Nellie knows much, yet he, like most of the other characters in the book, is searching for something he calls by the wrong name, probing the earth under the ranch for the hidden treasure of the bandit Joaquín Murieta with some gizmo with switches and dials. It is the nature of such treasures in the folklore of the West to constantly elude the searcher if he is found to be morally wanting:

---

31 Bergon takes up the issue of diminishing water and the poisoning of the Valley's water and soil in the chapter entitled "Drought in the Garden of the Sun" in his collection of essays *Two-Buck Chuck & The Marlboro Man* (Reno: University of Nevada Press, 2019). See also Marc Reisner's classic book *Cadillac Desert: The American West and Its Disappearing Water* (1986; New York, Penguin Books, 1993, revised edition), esp. 150-152.

the holes Nellie digs that pockmark the ranch are testaments to the way he, and all the characters in the book, and we ourselves, fall short. Love has become tangled in jealousy, betrayal, and rage. Violence has destroyed Sonny's body and has killed his best friend. But there may be grace. Grace, Father Dan, Sonny's confessor has told him, strikes like lightning, but you have to be ready.[32] You cannot finally discover it in the violent pleasures of a good fight or of a sexual conquest. You cannot find it with wires or dials. Like the life-giving water he watches pumping out of the ground on peaceful nights, the treasure is there, right under Sonny's feet, right under ours. We have only to be ready for it.

Works Cited

Bakhtin, Mikhail Mikhailovich. *The Dialogic Imagination: Four Essays by M. M. Bakhtin.* Edited by Michael Holquist. Translated by Caryl Emerson and Michael Holquist. Austin: University of Texas Press, 1981.

Bergon, Frank. *Jesse's Ghost.* Berkeley, CA: Heyday, 2011.

Dunbar-Ortiz, Roxanne. *Red Dirt: Growing Up Okie.* 1997. Norman: University of Oklahoma Press, 2006.

Gregory, James N. *American Exodus: The Dust Bowl Migration and Okie Culture in California.* New York: Oxford University Press, 1989.

Haslam, Gerald. *Haslam's Valley.* Berkeley, CA: Heyday Books, 2005.

Lange, Dorothea, and Paul Schuster Taylor. *An American Exodus.* 1939. New Haven: Yale University Press for the Oakland Museum, 1969.

O'Neal, Hank. *A Vision Shared: A Classic Portrait of America and Its People, 1935-1943.* New York: St. Martin's Press, 1976.

---

32 *Jesse's Ghost*, 18.

Frank Bergon: Dreaming the American West

David Means

Autobiographical Fuel

It's important to be reminded again and again that an author's life is the central conduit—no matter how much the author might deny it—through which creative visions flow. A boy is born in Ely, Nevada, on February 24, 1943. When he is five years old, his father moves the family to Madera County in California's San Joaquin Valley, where he grows up on a ranch, tending his father's livestock, working irrigation ditches, and, presumably, reading books on the side. This young man attends Bellarmine College Prep in San Jose, California, where he begins writing poetry and fiction. His first trip east is to Boston College, where he studies English, absorbing the voices of Robert Frost, T.S. Eliot, and Katherine Anne Porter among others, and he begins to write seriously, guided, for a few years, by the Irish writer Sean O'Faolain.[1] One can only guess how this young man felt—a westerner with life on a ranch still composing his formative memories, walking the humid streets of Boston—but one can be sure that he felt the disequilibrium of being in an unfamiliar cultural landscape, and the complex dynamic—Quentin Compson at Harvard comes to mind—that comes from being separated from family of origin, from his formative landscape.

In 1965, Bergon then went west again, to Stanford, as a Stegner Fellow, where he wrote fiction and, under the influence of Wallace Stegner, begins to develop a consciousness of his own "western" identity.[2] Then he returned to the east again, back into the cold, stony heart of New England, to Harvard, where he dove headlong into the study of literature,

---

1   Gregory L. Morris, *Frank Bergon*, Western Writers Series, 126 (Boise, ID: Boise State University, 1997), 6-8.
2   Ibid., 6-7.

into academic discourse, and, with what can only be called the alchemical magic of creative luck, located Stephen Crane as a subject. He dug deep into Crane's style, his voice, his life, and shortly after receiving his doctorate, he published *Stephen Crane's Artistry*, in which he explained that Crane's style "most successfully duplicates immediate experience when he gives voice to perceptions that can have no voice of their own, when he dwells in that mute land between event and human consciousness of event."[3] At the time Frank wrote these words, he did not know that, a few years later, in his first novel, *Shoshone Mike*, he would find his own way into expressing a "mute land," a zone between historical facts, individual lives, and the landscape in which they transpired.

After receiving his Ph.D. from Harvard, he accepted a tenure-track position at Vassar College, a solidly Eastern institution with a storied past. Eventually, after yearly summer trips to Pagosa Springs, Colorado, he bought a cabin in Blanco Basin. Each summer, at the end of a semester, on the very last day, he got in his truck with his beloved wife, Holly, and their dogs and headed west, taking the long route through the south, and then up into Colorado Rockies. This is the dynamic at hand: a writer who has settled down in the east but grown up in the West, an expatriate of sorts, a person steeped in the study of western history and literature, gathering facts, who, when it comes to writing fiction, must allow himself to trust his imagination, to synthesize everything he had learned, to avoid the didactic, and to let the vivacity of his visions leap far beyond the facts at hand, fueled by the drift of his imagination.

The fiction writer operates in an intuitive dream mode. As Elaine Scarry has pointed out in her brilliant *Dreaming by the Book*, fiction writing is associated with daydreaming, but it is, of course, much more complicated. Scarry argues that "though we think of the imagination and the verbal arts as continuous, they are instead discontinuous. The verbal arts are at once counterfactual and counterfictional. Like the daydream, the verbal arts are counterfactual; both the daydream and the poem bring into being things not previously existing in the world. But the verbal arts are also counterfictional, displacing the ordinary attributes of imagining—its faintness, two-dimensionality, fleetingness, and dependence on volitional labor—with the vivacity, solidity, persistence, and givenness of the perceptible world."[4] The writer attempts to give the reader instructions on how to

---

3   Frank Bergon, *Stephen Crane's Artistry* (New York: Columbia University Press, 1975), 15.
4   Elaine Scarry, *Dreaming by the Book* (Princeton, NJ: Princeton University Press, 1999), 28.

see a fictive dream; the writer listens and looks and ponders and catches visions, and then, through drafting and revisions, through structure and form—in a counterfictional way—to fine turn these instructions. Bergon's visions—and visions is the correct word—were fed from both the historical West and a much more personal West—the trickster west of his 1950s boyhood. Beginning with *Shoshone Mike*, moving through the antic and comic narratives of *The Temptations of St. Ed & Brother S* and *Wild Game*, and ending in his most recent, *Jesse's Ghost*, his work has gravitated towards explorations of physical violence in western landscapes. I believe his visions have been fed by his personal life, growing up on a ranch at a particular time in history, when he was, presumably, aware of the strange feedback loop of the mythic west feeding itself into the contemporary moment; his academic research, particularly on Stephen Crane's western stories; his love of boxing; his admiration of Sam Shepard; his experiences as an amateur magician; his sense of a wider, cosmic time (and justice) informed by his indoctrination into the tenants of the Catholic faith. All these aspects of his life fed into those moments when he was conjuring the visions and then carefully revising in that counterfictional mode.

Richard Prince and Marlboro Man

One afternoon, a few years ago, I stood with Frank in the Guggenheim Museum and examined huge photographs of cowboys working in magnificent western landscapes, driving cattle, roping, resting beneath cottonwood trees, photographs made by Richard Prince, who "appropriated" the images of the Marlboro cigarette campaign. I don't think I knew at the time that Frank was a friend of the cowboy in those photographs, the original Marlboro Man, Darrell Winfield, but as we moved around the museum, I immediately got the sense that he didn't like the work. Prince had taken the photographs and blown the images up, and the results seemed majestic and stunning. While iconic, they also—because I was aware of the source, the massive Philip Morris ad campaign, images that I had seen a thousand times in magazines and on billboards—seemed to have a strange patina that made me aware of the inauthentic nature of the idea of the authentic.

Prince made a fortune, and his name in the art world, with these photographs. Frank grimaced as he gazed at the images.

In his essay, "The Marlboro Man," Frank unravels the true story of the man in Prince's photographs, Darrell Winfield. "At six feet one, with a square jaw, straight dry lips, and sky-blue eyes surrounded by razor-thin wrinkles, his features are those of the archetypal cowboy etched in whang leather. His weathered face and trademark mustache, imitated by so many cowboys as to become a commonplace in ranch country, are familiar even to those too young to remember him from TV commercials and billboards because they've seen him online or in museum exhibitions or other countries where cigarette commercials aren't banned."[5]

The playwright Sam Shepard even referred to the Marlboro Man in his play, *Fool for Love*, and then, ironically, after the playwright's death, was in turn described as the Marlboro Man of the Movies.[6] Yet Prince's appropriated image of the American cowboy seemed that day, at the museum, to be the end point of a historical and cultural process (where else could it go? Could you take a photo of one of his photos at the Guggenheim then resell it for a million dollars at Sotheby's?). Notice that in both of these passages, Bergon homes in on the ironic nature of appropriation, this cycle of media creations—mythic and powerful—being fed back into the identities of western folks. The cowboys see Winfield's mustache and begin sporting their own. Shepard—aware of this cycle— appropriates the Marlboro Man, or at least gives him a nod in an ironic gesture, and then the eager media, upon his death, uses the Marlboro Man as a tag to define Shepard. These are narrow examples of a much wider, much more complex dynamic—one that ranges across the history of the West, from the earliest days.

In his concise study, Gregory L. Morris has pointed out that the awareness of a dynamic of place and culture, a feeding of powerful myths into the contemporary moment is a major element of all of Bergon's work. Morris quotes from the introduction to an anthology, *Looking Far West: The Search for the American West in History, Myth, and Literature*, edited by Bergon and his friend Zeese Papanikolas: "Again and again, the West shows that when a state of mind finds expression in action, myth becomes history, just as history is always aspiring to become myth."[7] This aspect of western life, this feedback loop—dime-novel tales, stories of

5   Frank Bergon. "West of California: The Marlboro Man," in *Two Buck Chuck & The Marlboro Man: The New Old West.* (Reno: University of Nevada Press, 2019), 201-252.
6   Ibid., 201-252.
7   Frank Bergon and Zeese Papanikolas, eds., *Looking Far West: The Search for the American West in History, Myth, and Literature* (New York: New American Library, 1978), 11.

outlaws, and, more recently, television and film narratives—feeding into the identities of western folks while they, in turn, provide more gist for novels, movies, television. Bergon locates this dynamic in his early academic work on Stephen Crane. In his introduction to *The Western Writings of Stephen Crane*, he notes: "Frontiersmen apparently began imitating their mythic counterparts as early as the eighteenth century when, according to the biography by John Bakeless, the real Daniel Boone began to model his public pronouncements on those of the fictional Daniel Boone as portrayed in 1784 by John Filson in *The Discovery, Settlement, and Present State of Kentucky*.[8] Through his academic studies, Bergon became highly attuned to this sometimes ironic, complex dynamic. Most of the characters in *Shoshone Mike* and *Jesse's Ghost* seem to be moving inside this dynamic, often aware that they are playing a part. Even Mike himself, a Native American, seems aware: "All the time you make up Indian words and tell us they're our words. We're not children. We have our own words that tell us how thing have always been."[9]

Bill Denio, the owner of the homestead and staging area of the posse going after Shoshone Mike, admits he's seen Indians roving the country but no more than usual. He describes the contemporary Indians: "They all dressed like any other buckaroos, and after working with them for a while, the men didn't even think of them as Indians. It was hard to imagine those men massacring anyone or living in the camp the men had found in the canyon. The massacre and camp resembled stories—old-timers used to tell when the men were kids."[10]

I'll go out on a limb and claim it's highly likely that Bergon became intuitively aware of the western feedback dynamic loop long before he headed east to Boston to study literature. Growing up on a ranch in the 1950s, surrounded by radio music, by films, by technological advances, he was highly attuned—as any westerner must be—to the cultural dynamic at hand. Surrounded by tough kids, seeing fistfights, boxing with his father, he gathered material—and questions—that would fuel his future creative work. I would guess—still out on the limb—that Frank was, when he began to create fiction, searching for the stability, a locus where he could render fictions that somehow reordered and revealed aspects of his own experience and, in turn, his own identity. Perhaps these fictional moments, in a paradoxical way, fed into who he became, and who he is now, in a kind

---

8   Frank Bergon, *The Western Writings of Stephen Crane* (New York: Signet, 1979), 11.
9   Frank Bergon, *Shoshone Mike* (New York: Viking Penguin, 1987), 67.
10 Ibid., 159.

of personal feedback loop that allowed him to make, after many years and several novels, the transition from the historical to the deeply personal, drawing directly, in his latest novel, *Jesse's Ghost*, from his own youth. Again, it seems important—going back to our day at the Guggenheim together—that in the case of wider historical aspects of Western culture, it is impossible, outside of fiction, to locate the starting point, the origination point. Somewhere, buried in some indefinable moment in history, lost to time, the first Mexican gaucho inspired someone else to replicate a certain look, his clothing, his moves, and, in turn, passed that image forward until the fashion of the cowboy was born. With Winfield—an origination point of a massive ad campaign that actually did feed into the way westerners saw themselves, Bergon got lucky. But, again, it is possible that knowing Winfield (Winfield worked on his father's ranch) helped him see into the nature of the West in a new way.

One question I would like to pose—and perhaps this was a subtext of my experience with Frank at the Guggenheim Museum that afternoon, perhaps even the subtext of Richard Prince's work—is where does the cultural feedback loop terminate within a fictive narrative? I'd argue that, in Frank's visions, this loop terminates inside acute moments of violence that reduce narrative to the binary physicality of win or lose, life or death. In Frank's work, scenes of violence function as moments of stasis surrounded by the retrospective moments of solitude and isolation and, sometimes, pastoral beauty. In a novel the reader is aware of all of the other narrative material around the scene she is reading.

That afternoon, as we walked together in the museum looking at the Prince photos we, too, were looking into frozen moments of stasis, captured images that were, however fake, however appropriated, surrounded by the narrative materials of our own life, and our friendship. Perhaps Frank was repelled, in part, by the violence of photography itself, capturing staged images of his friend. That day, Frank's grimace when looking at Prince's photographs of his friend was partly rooted, I believe, in his deep mission as an artist to locate the truth as much as possible, to respect reality. Reality was not in the fake images conjured up by Philip Morris and a team of ad executives, designers, and photographers, but a real man—his friend—named Darrell Winfield who lived on his own ranch in a double-wide trailer and was in opposition to the "legendary cowboys, who battled Indians in fiction and film," and was married to Lennie, a member of the Choctaw tribe.[11] (Winfield's ranch was surrounded by the Wind River Reservation.)

---

11   Frank Bergon, *Two Buck Chuck & The Marlboro Man*, 201-252.

Again, these photographs were a betrayal not only of his friend but of his own sense of artistic mission—his own credo, which was to seek out as much as possible the truth, to stick as close as possible to the facts, and then to take the artistic leap into creating fiction of verisimilitude.

Magic, the Practical Joke, and the Fistfight

In Bergon's world, cowboys are trick players and tricksters. "They constantly pulled tricks on each other, or on us, wanting to bet on anything. Like as not, a cowboy would bet the sun wouldn't come up in the morning, not caring he'd lose so long as he got you riled up with some kind of bluff. That's what Jesse liked about them, how far they'd go to play a joke on someone."[12] A few sentences later, not by coincidence, Darrell Winfield makes his cameo as a character named Duane. "He wore chaps and a straw hat, like he always did in the summer until Mitch's daddy sold the ranch and Duane moved to Wyoming, where the Marlboro people found him and got him started appearing in commercials."[13]

Sometimes an external reality—brutal, random—can be controlled or diminished into the linguistic structure of the joke, or through the actions of a trickster. Even the practical joke—turned physical—is fundamentally rooted in language, in the aftermath, in the retelling of past humiliations.

Fistfighting in Bergon's fictive world—like a joke—is momentary, often unrelated to external grudges, sometimes spontaneous, and usually meaningless beyond the context of the fight itself. Fistfighting is, for the most part, a matching of skills and a blunt, mostly brutal form of expression that is self-contained; the fight transpires within the frame of the action itself and seems, inside the narrative moment, to have little to do with larger structures—although of course, for a reader, it does. Ultimately, it is a codified test of wills, and what is carried forward for the winner, and for Jesse, are the bragging rights, the retelling of the win, and for the loser, a silence that seems to mirror the landscape—somehow signifying the brutality of chance in the nature of the western mind, as clear and frank as a glyph on the wall of a canyon

---

12 Frank Bergon, *Jesse's Ghost* (Berkeley, CA: Heyday, 2011), 55.
13 Ibid., 56.

Practical magic was an early interest of Bergon's.[14] As a teenager he was a serious magician and even performed a few paying gigs. Magic—like the practical joke—is rooted in the physical, in the eye and hand, in the nature of the body—and it operates retroactively. The person fooled, tricked by sleight of hand and control of eye, retells the experience and in the retelling, the rehashing—how did he do that? What did he do to make me see that? How did he get out of that bind?—feels implicated in the trick and, in turn, I'd argue, into a new orientation towards the nature of "reality." Frank's sense of physicality, his interest in magic, and his interest in boxing, have fed his vision of what violence on the personal, codified level can mean.

In the fistfight—or even in the chaos of the chaotic fight between Shoshone Mike and the posse—narrative time enters a stasis of sorts, and everything within the scene becomes determined by the violence itself. This is important—in relation to Bergon's wider narrative structures—because the structures themselves, and all of the scenes they contain, resonate around these scenes of violence in the retroactive nature of fiction itself.

In *Shoshone Mike*, Bergon moves from character to character and shifting points of view, reorienting the reader with historical documents, newspaper accounts. (This introduction of documents—two detailed maps, the newspaper account of the double murder at Imlay, a long letter from a prosecuting attorney in Idaho, and even the afterword in which Bergon comments on the sources and method of creating his book, are literary sleights of hand, flashing cards in a way to distract the reader from the imagined visions for a moment, creating a liminality that amplifies the overall power of the imagined scenes, forcing the reader directly into the vortex of history.) *Jesse's Ghost* operates with a different trick, slowly spiraling back in time again and again from the present moment—fueled by Sonny's voice—and breaking up the narrative in a way that thickens the reader's sense of history.

Sam Shepard

Frank has mentioned many times over the years in our conversations that the playwright Sam Shepard is one of the best—perhaps even the best—contemporary western writers. Shepard was an admixture of writer,

---

14   Personal interview with Frank Bergon.

cosmopolitan movie star, trickster rock and roller, who embodied in his work and in his life all of the paradoxes—the destabilized, postmodern sense that identity was fluid, and yet also wrote thrilling plays that seemed, in their tense dynamics to locate, at least aesthetically, the "true West." Shepard grew up in Duarte, California, about 22 miles northeast of downtown Los Angeles. Although his father had a few avocado trees, and as a teenager Shepard joined Future Farmers of America, the local 4-H club, and worked on a ranch during his summer break, his upbringing seems more suburban than western.[15] Yet he grew up—literally—on the edge of the western landscape. Like the characters in his play, *True West*, in which one brother is a Hollywood screenwriter and the other is a drifter who occasionally goes to the desert to live, the complexity of Shepard's personality seems to have arisen from the flux of several worlds, an imagined "real West" of men on horses and cowboys and working the land, and another, much more intellectual, urban source that includes rock and roll, films.

Born the same year as Shepard, Bergon's vision is similar, and his characters—not to mention Winfield—Sonny in *Jesse's Ghost*, or Sheriff Lamb, could easily slip into a role in a Shepard play. They too are caught in the flux of history and culture, trying to nail down the "true West." As writers, Shepard and Bergon are as much at home in the East Coast, on the streets of New York, in museums and attending plays, as they are in the West. There is a deep, internal, personal dynamic at play between their contemporary sensibilities and their awareness of the historical West.

In his introduction to *Fool for Love and Other Plays*, Ross Wetzsteon calls Shepard's characters "shaman figures—those pop heroes embodying our national obsessions, cowboys, criminals, rock stars—who confront the psychic traumas that result when the integrity of the self comes into conflict with the compromises of community."[16] The characters in *Jesse's Ghost* are also shaman figures, moving through Sonny's memory and reminiscences, vacillating between past and present. Written in a counterpoint of flashbacks, the novel traces the history of Jesse and the narrator, Sonny, weaving back into time to their youth on the ranch in Madera and then forward into the contemporary moment, unfolding, gradually, the story of Jesse's murder at the hands of the narrator, and in doing so, revealing, in a kind of counterpoint, the tensions between past and present realities. The novel feels deeply personal, drawing from Bergon's

---

15   John J. Winters, *Sam Shepard: A Life* (Berkeley, CA: Counterpoint, 2017), 31-35.
16   Ross Wetzsteon, "Introduction," in *Sam Shepard: Fool for Love and Other Plays* (New York: Dial Press, 2006), 5.

own early life on a ranch rich details of the workings of irrigation pumps, the attempted vegetables patch, the financial stress, while also painting an elegiac portrait of summer days spent working hard and playing hard. In a particularly beautiful and vivid scene in the book, Sonny is "changing up" the irrigation:

> After I again changed my water in the alfalfa field at around one in the morning, Jesse was still in the pick-up with Sonia. I watched the moon come up over the Sierras—a mountain range I couldn't see but knew to be there because of how the moon popped into view higher than the valley horizon. It was a half-moon, almost three-quarters, silvery but less pale than in early summer. Moonlight brightened the ditch water creeping over the ground like slow-moving mercury as it twisted around the alfalfa stalks, giving the air a sweet, musty smell. You could almost hear the water crackle through the hay stubble. I liked irrigating at night when it was quiet and peaceful this way, and I liked it much better than when I traded off with Jesse and climbed onto the Jeep pulling the rackety hay bailer. Waiting to bale hay wasn't so bad, though. I'd stretch out in the hay field and lay my hand on top of the windrow so that when the dew came in, the wetness would wake me.[17]

Could anyone imagine so vividly a night working the irrigation if they hadn't done it themselves? I doubt it. A page later, Sonny is still working—and still gazing, casting his eye over the night world of the ranch. Now he's looking and thinking, and we're thinking with him, drawn into a profound moment of stasis—aware in only a slight way that we are moving through a reminiscence, aware of the fistfights, the violence in previous scenes, but also aware, because of the precision of the details—in the paradox of great fiction—that we are simply inside Sonny's youthful mind.

> I wish I could understand what I was doing out there. I don't mean what I was doing in the field of alfalfa stubble—I was irrigating hay to make it grow. I knew

---

17   *Jesse's Ghost*, 124.

that—but what the hay and myself were even doing out
there on an August night in the San Joaquin Valley under
a tilted moon. It was something I couldn't figure. Why
wasn't I someone else? It stumped me why I wasn't one
of Duane's cows in the feedlot or the wet gopher that
Dewey had pulled from a ditch by the tail and wacked
in the head with the sharp point of his pocketknife,
then laughed that wheezy laugh of his while the gopher
wiggled around from its tail pinched between Dewey's
fingers, flinging blood all over the place. I could've been,
I suppose, a gopher or a cow, just like Sonia could've
been a fox, not a girl. Or not born at all. Any of us. Or
like my momma told me when she was drunk how she
could've strangled me when I was born.[18]

This voice of a young western kid, of someone alone in the night speaking
to himself, mirrors Shepard's famous soliloquies. The narrative steps
outside and away from violence and ruminates on larger issues, and yet,
somehow, in the quiet, there is a reference to the violence. And here we
have a western kid waxing poetically—in his own way—into the deepest
existential question. Surrounding this moment, of course, as it is drawn
up out of the well of Sonny's memory (and the reader has this awareness
of that particular psychic subsurface), is the violence of Jesse's death,
ahead in the narrative. And rotating around this scene, like navigational
stars, are the fistfights that mark the narrative.

Boxing

In her classic study, *On Boxing*, Joyce Carol Oates opens her book with the
lines: "No other subject is, for the writer, so intensely personal as boxing.
To write about boxing is to write about oneself—however elliptically, and
unintentionally. And to write about boxing is to be forced to contemplate

18   Ibid., 126.

not only boxing, but the perimeters of civilization—what it is, or should be, to be 'human.' "[19] I'd argue that the same might be said for fistfighting, or even for the formation of a posse to hunt down a band of Native Americans. To write of formalized violence, of moments of codified action, is to somehow write of the self—for in the imagined experience of violence, in order to dream into an evocative vision of the events, one can only draw from an inner, intimate relation with the nature of physicality. Bergon has a love of boxing—he is a fan, and he taught a famous course in 1994 and 1996 on the subject at Vassar College, bringing in Floyd Patterson and Oates to speak. In the course, "Reading the Fights: Boxing and American Values," Frank and his colleague, the historian Benjamin Kohl, used boxing as a lens through which to view "American values and problems—like racism [and] notions of masculinity."[20] Again, as a writer, he is aware that it is impossible to separate boxing, or any form of violence, from the culture surrounding it, using it as a tool through which to examine other aspects of his characters' lives. But he also understands— as does Oates—that fighting itself, at least boxing, and the fistfights in *Jesse's Ghost*, are unique closed systems.

The violence of fistfighting—at least in California during the 1950s—wasn't just about proving masculine power, at least not in the narratives created around it, but, I'd argue, more about the nature of time in relation to the events; the way the fight fit into the larger narrative, and the intensity of the story of each fight, as it was lived out second by second behind some tavern outside Sacramento, or in the ring in Las Vegas. Hemingway, and then Mailer, lay claim to the sport as somehow mirroring their own interests in courage, as part of a ritual rooted in masculine testing, but Bergon's interest in violence, in fighting, is rooted in much wider concerns. Jesse does fight to "prove his manhood," but it is only a minor aspect of his reasoning.

Unlike the posse in *Shoshone Mike*—formed slowly, over the course of several days, and responding, in part, to newspaper accounts of events, fueled by racial prejudice and cross-cultural misunderstandings, the fistfights in *Jesse's Ghost* simply arrive out of everyday life, are part of the landscape of time, and outside of the contemporary moment and therefore historical judgment. Whereas the violence in *Shoshone Mike*, seen through time and through history, seems to be the accumulation of much wider, yet

---

19   Joyce Carol Oates, "Foreword," in *On Boxing* (1987; New York: Harper Perennial, 2006), vii.
20   Frank Bergon, "Boxing at Vassar," *Vassar Quarterly* 108, no. 1 (Winter 2012): 14.

infinitely precise misjudgment, injustice, racism—powerful forces of fear betraying the human heart. What becomes clear in both of these dynamics is that Bergon has internalized, through his love of boxing, and his acute attention to historical records, the nature of violence and the different shapes it can take.

Imagining Against the Facts

When Sonny, the narrator of *Jessie's Ghost*, backtracks over events that led him to kill his friend Jesse, telling his story to his old friend Mitch—a writer—a process that takes the entire narrative—as he closes in on his final confession, driving with Mitch, he stops short when he gets to the seminal moment of the shooting, unable to go on with that part of his story. Only later, when Mitch has finished writing an article about the event, and Sonny hears Mitch read it aloud, are we made privy to the entire tragic story. This is telling because it mirrors the use of newspaper accounts and reportage in *Shoshone Mike*. A story needs to be translated into facts, or what seem like facts, into reportage, and then transmuted through the imagination into narrative fiction. This reflects Bergon's own deep process. He must locate, as often as possible, factual events. He must find the truth first, and then he can leap into fiction. History is entwined, twisted up in personal narrative, a retelling—listened to by participants, who then double back to look for the truth. The article, a formal, nonfiction reportage of past events in a logical form, allows Sonny to reveal his story. Journalism in the form of newspaper articles; historical documents; written history, are all tools—both in reality and in the imagined creations of Bergon—to act as a catalyst for the envisioning of truth in the form of narrative. It might be argued that westerners do this on a daily level. The actions at Ruby Ridge, the more recent Bundy standoff, or, going farther back in history, the story of Jesse James, or Daniel Boone—all reported in print, or more recently on the internet, have served to catalyze countless western narratives. In her recent memoir, *Educated*, Tara Westover, raised by radical survivalist Mormons in Idaho, recalls how her father obsessed about the shootout at Ruby Ridge, telling and retelling and reshaping the story, and the way she felt, later, attending Brigham Young, when she heard the "true" facts of the story.[21] This is a fundamental dynamic at play in Bergon's creative process—searching

---

21   Tara Westover, *Educated: A Memoir* (New York: Random House, 2018).

as far as possible into the facts and then, in turn, building a fictive vision that goes beyond them into credible verisimilitude.

Jesse's Ghost and *Shoshone Mike* are both narratives of violent trauma—one a wider historical trauma that radiates outward in time—one final massacre of Native Americans in an event fueled by speculative rumor, cultural misunderstandings, and mythic archetypes. In *Jesse's Ghost* the history of the West floats outside; the wider history of the West is drawn into the precise lives of characters through time.

Jesse and his friends fight the Hell's Angels, a California-born street gang, when they arrive from outside. They strike a defiant pose, sticking up for their rights to the landscape they claim as their own, and only this fight in the novel—shown mainly from a wider vantage—seems rooted in a more complex social dynamic, whereas the casual fistfights, often on the spur of the moment, seem to collapse into their own physicality, being a rudimentary matter of brutal—almost pure—physicality. Yet the reader—aware of the form of the novel, sensing the reminiscent quality, aware of the love Sonny has for Jesse, for his memory of the past—can't help but be aware of something else: Sonny is willfully, through his retelling, his sharing with Mitch, turning Jessie into an iconic hero of his own past, a young man who was utterly fearless, highly attractive to everyone, with a quick, easy smile. The love one feels radiating out of Sonny seems—it would be safe to say—the love he feels not only for his past, for the ranch in California, but also his love of those boys, his friends, who struggled to internalize and to find a way through the unspoken historical tropes that were floating around them at all times, the cowboys who appeared on the ranch with their silly tricks, the drunks on the road, the brutal violence, reflects the tender care and love for the past that inspired Bergon to create Sonny in the first place.

Historical Flux and the Inner Life of Bergon's Characters

Narrative history lies, paradoxically, between two points: one point is the irrevocable facts, dates and times, movements and geographical locations. The other point resides inside the emotional resonance of each individual in narrative time—individual characters inside individual predicaments as time flows behind and ahead. When the physical frontier was settled, when, at least symbolically, the wilderness had been conquered, a dynamic shifted. As Erik Erikson notes in "The Frontier and the American Identity," one of the selections in *Looking Far West: The Search for the American West in History, Myth, and Literature*, edited by Bergon and his friend Zeese Papanikolas, there was a time when an adage was commonly heard in the West: "If you can see your neighbor's chimney, it is time to move on."[22] To be a westerner is to be filled with an intensely willed desire for isolation and privacy. But what happens when via technology, telegraph machines at first and now, years later, the internet and satellite dishes, all chimneys are symbolically visible? I would argue that the concepts of isolation and solitude are forced inward. In other words, western literature—at least literature that is highly attuned to the realities that Bergon has discovered—must somehow move inward, into the identity of each character—surrounded, still, by the hardscrabble landscape, and history, of the West. How does one write a true western narrative with this new metaphysical arrangement? This is the question Frank had to confront each time he sat down to write. Like all artists, he was faced with an infinite number of choices and had to rely on his gut, his intuition. He did not set off down the Cormac McCarthy path, spinning histories that rarely go inward, taking his characters on long, drawn-out, often violent journeys into the desolation of finely rendered historical landscapes. Instead, he drew from the cultural moment—and from his place straddling the East and the West—and, as Hunter Thompson did in his trickster gonzo approach in *Fear and Loathing* (which I'd argue is a western, with its desert setting and its trickster outlaw tropes), or as James Welsh did in *Fools Crow* (making us privy, through language, to the inner lives of Native Americans)—he moved inward. It's important to note that Bergon is a product of the late 1960s and early 1970s. When Thomas Pynchon's published *Gravity's Rainbow*, he sent his Vassar students to go down to the local bookstore and buy it in hardcover. They read it together. "You had to be there!" he exclaimed, when I asked him what he thought of the book.[23] Bergon found unique, contemporary ways to combine the wide view—historical facts (the opening of the railhead in Kansas), cultural facts (gauchos inspired cowboy fashion)—with the imagined internal lives of his characters, and in doing, exposing in his own way the relationship between the western landscape and the inner lives.

---

22   *Looking Far West*, 236.
23   Personal interview.

Cosmic Time, Violence, and Justice

Shoshone Mike is a masterpiece because it poetically incorporates historical facts—the feedback loop of culture, the dynamic of geographic distances and inner distances—with aesthetic grace. It's important to know that this grace is an elemental aspect of Bergon's work and his life. He gracefully lucked upon a subject that mirrored his own life—a band of Native Americans, the last to be massacred, who wandered a path that mirrored his own geographic history. He opens his arms to the contemporary culture with a graceful embrace. Although Bergon shirks discussing his indoctrination into the Catholic Church—at least with me—it is clear that his extraordinary sense of time as it relates to violence and justice comes from a sense of devotion (and vocation), if not to the doctine of the church, then at least to what might be called the cosmology of Christianity. Or, if this makes the reader comfortable, in a more general sense that time flows in all directions out of the power of the individual spirit as it relates to some greater, perhaps even imagined order and, someplace ahead, a terminal moment of cosmic justice. For example, in *Jesse's Ghost*, Sonny finds solace in Father Dan:

> Some people think I became a Catholic because of Lynette, but it was really the priest I met when doing my time. I had to become something. I couldn't live alone with what I'd done. This priest—Father Dan—grew up in Coalinga, where his daddy worked in the oil fields, so we had a valley connection. His weathered face carried that sad, tired look you see in oil-field workers as he showed me the direct line stretching from the Church today all the way back to when Jesus told Simon Peter, "You are the rock upon which I will build my church." Sure, it's full of failing, but that's the whole point. The blood of the Lamb doesn't just wash everything away, how other churches say. Even Peter betrayed his best friend, denied he ever knew him in the Garden of Agony and did nothing to stop the Romans from killing him. Jesus forgave him, but Peter suffered for it all the rest of his life.[24]

---

24 *Jesse's Ghost*, 4.

Bergon gives his character his own Garden of Agony—the novel itself—and isn't asking for forgiveness. In all of his work there are moments of pastoral beauty and solitude that reveal that he is drawing on his early church experiences and is not only aware of the nature of justice and time, but also the grace that time is bestowing. In *Shoshone Mike*, Father Enright is having a crisis of faith that allows the narrative, again, to open up into a wider cosmology. After the massacre, he preaches to his congregation—and to the reader—and he turns to St. Paul. "St. Paul did not live outside time. Time was all he had," Enright says.[25] Inside the sacred space of the church—and in Father Enright's mind—there is another sense of western time. Bergon—through Enright—further elucidates St. Paul's teachings: "I want justice, you say, not charity. But there is no difference. To love our neighbor is to treat him with justice, to love our enemy is to treat him with justice."[26] Bergon's placement of these passages, after the complex struggle Father Enright has with his own faith earlier in the book, serves to prod the reader to ponder the meaning, arriving from the juxtaposition of so many points of view, as it relates to time outside of history, pushing one to consider the nature of cosmic time, of some potential final judgment.

This aspect of Frank's personality—and here I must get personal—this moral center, this core of goodness, can be seen in the way he devoted himself to teaching, his loving care for his students, his grace as a friend. His early indoctrination as a Catholic—tempered, as with James Joyce, by acute skepticism, perhaps even what might seem to be disbelief—has served his imagination, allowing imagined scenes of violence to play out within a wider sense of cosmic time.

In a scene near the end of the novel, in a short chapter, Father Enright speaks with Sheriff Lamb and says, "We said they were savages. We said they were going to destroy our homes, our families, our laws, everything that made us people. Then we went and did that to them. We did to them exactly what we said they were going to do to us. What does that make us?"[27] The chapter ends at that point, leaving the reader with the silence of the empty page but also, because we have been listening to Enright, a sense that there might be, somewhere out there, at some endpoint—imagined or real—a moment of real justice, when all narrative time curls up into the warm embrace of the truth. The chapter ends and we carry those thoughts—for a few seconds, a day, however long it takes to turn the

---

25   *Shoshone Mike*, 228.
26   Ibid., 230.
27   Ibid., 269.

page—to the next chapter, which opens in landscape. "High dust clouds streaked the horizon as the last bands of sheep crossed the desert toward the shearing corrals. At the makeshift pens near the Western Pacific freight house at the end of town, Nellie Lamb climbed from an automobile with three men in business suits to watch the shearers at work."[28]

Between Father Enright's utterance and the firmness, the solidity of the image at the beginning of the next chapter, hovering in there—for the sensitive reader—is an aspect of mystery that contains the deeper mystery of existence, one that Bergon, through his imaginative power (and his structuring of the book, its parataxis), resonates grace. Or perhaps it would be better to put it this way: love. This is the place where history ends and fiction begins and, touching the "real" lives of readers, continues on. There are no answers within the visions a writer creates, but there are questions that double into themselves so deeply that they provide something that feels like an answer: a sense that there is meaning in the disparate—not Newtonian cause and effect, as we all know, but quantum—leaps. A chapter ends, gracing us with silence until the next scene begins.

Inside the silence, the empty space between the pages, is the tragedy of western history entwined with its glories; one sits alongside the other eternally, and all we can do—Frank's vision as an artist says, the way he has lived his life says—is tweeze apart and listen carefully to the silence.

Frank, the Man

As a fiction writer I hope to never betray the power of imagined work by claiming it can be connected piecemeal with its creator. (I attempted to do it in this essay, but it goes against the grain of my creative spirit.) In the end I resort to memories of times with Frank and his wife, Holly, sitting in his backyard while he cooks steaks, listening to him talk as he churns ice cream; watching him load chunks of wood into his stove in his old house across the Hudson River from Vassar College (it felt symbolically important that Frank lived on the west bank of the Hudson, keeping the river between his life as a writer and Vassar College), a house that, each time I entered it, reminded me of the photographs of Wright Morris, the stately austerity and solidity of a prairie farmhouse; or the times we sat on the campus smoking our annual cigar, rehashing the year, talking

---

28 Ibid., 270.

about life, about writing, about writers we loved or despised, and I heard him criticize a particular aspect of one of Cormac McCarthy's novels, or his take on Joan Didion's Okie blind spot, as only someone personally invested in the West, as a man who knows how to bridle a horse, who knows the nooks and crannies of that landscape, who understands what it feels like to be labeled an outsider, who had grappled with his Basque identity and negotiated the tightrope stretched between academic study of the West and imagining the West. One winter afternoon, I stood beside Frank while we watched a pro boxer hit the heavy bag and laughed as we tried to describe the sound—the surprisingly loud wallop of force—and I understood that he was searching for something inside the scene we were witnessing, not as an academic, but as a writer looking for sparks, for something to feed his vision. Another time, at a Bob Dylan concert, wending our way up to the stage later in the show, after the disgruntled audience had cleared out, we stood at Dylan's feet as he played a keyboard and I felt the same thing. We were two writers together, looking closely, gathering images. Once when I was driving somewhere with Frank, he put a CD into the player: Bob Dylan's *Pat Garrett & Billy the Kid.* I felt a sense that within Dylan's voice—within the fact that the music had been written for a film, which in turn was a mythologized version of something already mythologized—there might be a spark. (Note: Everything a writer does, every action, every, single moment in life feeds the muse, and the writer is highly aware of this fact as he moves through the mundane, everyday requirements of life.)

Another time, after Frank and his beautiful wife, Holly, moved to Martha's Vineyard, I was poking around and saw a stack of books about California history, and on the top of the stack was *Autobiography of a Brown Buffalo* by Oscar Zeta Acosta, Hunter Thompson's sidekick on his trickster adventures in Las Vegas, a lawyer and Chicano rights activist who disappeared in Mexico. Somehow, this particular book seemed to be a clue to the mystery of Frank as a creative soul. It told me he was a man who is wide open in the search.

One night, on Martha's Vineyard, driving along the water, I listened as he recited from memory the opening of Wallace Steven's poem, "The Idea of Order at Key West," and I heard, in his tone, the relishing of the words, his love of language, of Stevens, and his admiration of certain sensibilities. We were driving along the coast and the water was glinting with light and matched the music of the words—and in that moment, I think I felt the eastern aspect of Frank's vision, his rootedness on the island, and the beautiful enigmatic tension that makes up a creative life. The imagination—I felt—is powerful. It's a tool that many fail to understand. The power of Frank's imagination has allowed him to return to the source, his boyhood ranch in California, his birthplace in Ely, Nevada, and his grandmother's Basque Hotel in Battle Mountain.

Early in our friendship, I read *Shoshone Mike*, on a trip home to Michigan, leaning against the wall in my childhood bedroom, and I breathed a sigh of relief because it was a masterpiece, a perfect book, a novel that combined form and history and narrative into a unique, symphonic, paratactic experience: each section, each chapter, resonating with the others in retrospect to reveal the paradox, the truth, of both history and individual life; that it is simply indescribable except through art itself, through the confrontation with a paradox of truths playing off of each other, so that even the settlers who joined the posse, each one feeling in that moment feeling one way or another in the horrific action—although later shifting views—felt justified; just as Jesse, inside his fights, lived only for the next punch. Reading that night, I felt joy in the fact that Frank was a gifted fiction writer—someone who could fling himself far beyond his academic knowledge of the world, someone who could live both inside his life and outside it at the same time. Above all Frank is committed to love and truth. He is someone who has given the world his gifts, in many forms, as a scholar, a teacher, and, above all, an artist of the highest order. The gift he has given me is the gift of friendship.

I'm not an academic, I'm a fiction writer. Trying to tweeze apart the sources of these creative visions—to compose a formal academic study of two of his novels, *Shoshone Mike* and *Jesse's Ghost*, which seemed to me to form bookends around his large creative project—I found myself drawing various connections, many of which have already been made before by brilliant scholars. Another factor was my love of Frank and Holly. I could not pull myself away from all of the time I had spent with him, with my sense that to tweeze apart his work in a scholarly manner would be to betray it somehow.

Fiction writing is a form of daydreaming, but it is much more than that. Many readers—even academics—fail to understand that the process itself takes a giving in, a release, from information and facts while, at the same time—and this is the impossible paradox—a drawing on the author's part from all facts, from all the information collected by the author in the past. Fiction is a controlled magic trick; fiction does come from dreaming, from conjuring up visions, but these visions are then translated into text that—through careful revision—gives the reader just enough instructive material through which to see. In his fiction—from *Shoshone Mike* to *Jesse's Ghost*—Frank has, one way or another, discovered aesthetic techniques that have allowed him to risk creating fiction that leaps beyond his own life, beyond the facts into visions of the West that stand up to the demands of rereading. He has found his own way to probe the infinite vastness of the contemporary and historical West, to create a body of literary work in his own, distinctive voice that is a significant contribution to the canon of western literature. It is a voice that refuses to avoid the truth. It is a voice that is determined to respect history—his own and that of those who are lost to the past. It is voice that touches upon the enigmatically individual lives that once moved through the blunt reality of the historical West—submerged souls, devoured by time, who have been, it seems, given a new life in the wonderful characters who have bloomed full-blown from his vast imagination.

WORKS CITED

Bergon, Frank. "Boxing at Vassar." *Vassar Quarterly* 108, no. 1 (Winter 2012): 14-19.

———. "Introduction." In *The Western Writings of Stephen Crane*, edited by Frank Bergon, 1-27. New York: Signet, 1979.

———. *Jesse's Ghost*. Berkeley, CA: Heyday, 2011.

———. *Shoshone Mike*. New York: Viking Penguin, 1987.

———. *Stephen Crane's Artistry*. New York: Columbia University Press, 1975.

Bergon, Frank, and Zeese Papanikolas. Eds. *Looking Far West: The Search for the American West in History, Myth, and Literature*. New York: New America Library, 1978.

Morris, Gregory L. *Frank Bergon*. Western Writers Series, 126. Boise, ID: Boise State University, 1997.

Long Shadows Across the Valley: Regarding Difference, Work, and Community in Frank Bergon's California

Nancy S. Cook

Hey, you don't know me but you don't like me
Say you care less how I feel
'Cause how many of you that sit and judge me
Ever walked the streets of Bakersfield

—Homer Joy 1973[1]

In California's Central Valley agriculture shaped a culture both deeply diverse and socially hierarchical, while producing commodities for world export. Workers from around the world came to the Central Valley, and with each generation, some moved up the economic and social food chain, some slipped down, some were deported, some escaped, some hobbled away, looking for work elsewhere. In his writing about California Frank Bergon reads the ways in which legacies of difference have both lethal and redemptive consequences.

Bergon's work engages many kinds of difference: historical, hierarchical, perspectival, embodied, as it also posits the legacies of those differences as they play out in one small section of the Great Central Valley. My essay surveys Bergon's California writing, from individual essays to the 2011 novel *Jesse's Ghost,* to his recent essay collection *Two-Buck Chuck & The Marlboro Man: The New Old West,* examining the ways in which difference

---

1 Homer Joy, "Streets of Bakersfield," recorded by Buck Owens in 1972, then as a duet with Dwight Yoakam in 1988. The duet version reached number one on the Billboard Country charts and was a Grammy nominee for Best Country Song. By 1988, the version features an accordion and reveals a strong influence of Mexican musical traditions.

functions, with a focus on embodied difference, especially in terms of social class, in everyday life. For convenience and clarity, I will use the ethnic and racial terms used in the texts. Bergon uses such terms carefully, according to place, time, and character, so while many have passed out of polite discourse, they are an important part of his place-making techniques.

Frank Bergon's thinking about his life in the Great Central Valley, about his familial place-making there, and about the changes realized, all come to bear on his insistence that California claims an important role in the history of the American West. For Bergon, an attentive look at inland California reveals complexities often overlooked or suppressed in representations of the American West. The observations collected, the scholarly consideration, and the stories gleaned from a lifetime of study of the North American West figure prominently throughout his career. Even when his interest lies in the sweep of history, he grounds broad claims in the details of everyday life, as it is embodied in history's forgotten actors. For example, in a review of *Small Bird, Tell Me: Stories of Greek Immigrants in Utah,* Bergon praises author Helen Papanikolas for both her rendering of the everyday and the way she connects the lives of working-class immigrants to larger historical trends. He writes: "What these stories offer as fiction is how private lives intersect with public events. In these stories we come to know how it felt to be in the skin of the historical participants themselves." He adds that Papanikolas pulls no punches, for "[t]he stories don't always tell what the participants might like to hear."[2]

An insistence on the embodied experience of Central Valley residents from across a racial, ethnic, and class spectrum ignites Bergon's critique of Joan Didion. While a longtime admirer of her work, Bergon bristles at both her omissions and her caricatures of his Valley neighbors. "The great blind spot of her work," he writes, "is that she doesn't see beyond stereotypes the Dust Bowl refugees she went to school with or the many ways the original Okies and their sons and daughters altered the valley and the state."[3] For Bergon, Didion's failure to see how Okies changed California represents a bizarre omission, as she skips over the decades of the twentieth century that include significant migration of working-class poor from Oklahoma, Texas, and Arkansas. He points out that "[b]y 1950, Okies constituted thirteen percent of California's population and twenty-two percent of the San Joaquin Valley—statistics, it would seem,

---

2   Frank Bergon, "Review of *Small Bird, Tell Me: Stories of Greek Immigrants in Utah. By Helen Papanikolas (Athens: Swallow Press/Ohio University Press), 1993." Western American Literature* 30, no. 3 (Fall 1995): 295-296.

3   Frank Bergon, "Joan Didion's Forgotten Okies." Unpublished manuscript, 1.

noteworthy for Didion's book about California and its Central Valley."[4] While Okies are mentioned, in derogatory terms in both *Slouching Towards Bethlehem* and *The White Album*, they merit no discussion in her California collection *Where I Was From*. Bergon concludes that for Didion, Okies contribute to the overarching narrative of California's decline. "She grew up with the idea she acknowledges as romantic that California had been spoiled." For Didion, he writes:

> [c]hange meant decline, such as someone's choice, she says, to vacation on Maui rather than to take the cruise ship *Lurline* to the traditional Hawaiian destination of Honolulu. Another sign of decline was someone's choosing to go back east to college at Princeton rather than the traditional choice of Berkeley or Stanford. Further decline occurred with the breakup of big ranches into subdivisions with names like Rancho Del Rio No. 1 and Rancho Del Rio No. 3, filling with the descendants of "new people" her grandfather vilified.[5]

The old California landowners, the pioneer stock, has been supplanted by corporate developers and agribusiness. While land use statistics from the Central Valley don't support her claims, nevertheless it suits the declentionist narrative. "Her stance as a romantic Westerner in *Slouching Towards Bethlehem* and as a disappointed romantic in *Where I Was From*," Bergon finds, "gives edge to her vignettes of a California in decline, but exchanging one set of myths for another sustains a blind spot and creates, in her phrasing, a 'fable of confusion' about the details of social history and the realities of American social class keeping the children of California and the West—the children of America—disconnected."[6]

It is important for Bergon to show Didion's blindness, I think, in part because hers remains the dominant literary voice speaking critically of California, and the Okies and their descendants represent a portion of those Americans who feel voiceless and have become supporters of politicians like Donald Trump. Less measured than Bergon, I imagine a more aggressive intervention for Didion: I'd like to see her tormented by

4   Ibid., 4.
5   Ibid., 9.
6   Ibid., 13.

loudspeaker, à la Manuel Noriega, with a continuous loop of the Buck Owens and Dwight Yoakam duet of "Streets of Bakersfield." "You don't know me but you don't like me," they sing, with fiddle and accordion back-up, "Say you care less how I feel/'Cause how many of you that sit and judge me/Ever walked the streets of Bakersfield"?[7] While Frank Bergon refrains from taunting Joan Didion in this (or any other way), both *Jesse's Ghost* and *Two-Buck Chuck & the Marlboro Man* offer an important response to Didion's blindness, her prejudices, and her mythologies.

By the late 1950s, when the narrator of *Jesse's Ghost*, Wade "Sonny" Childers, was in junior high school, two generations of Okies, innumerable generations of "Mexicans," Issei, Nisei, and Sansei had taken turns as the reviled, deported, and interned underclasses in the Central Valley.

Those legacies persisted through the 1950s and into the 1960s, the historical terrain of the novel. The racial and ethnic diversity of the Valley is much more complex than I will suggest here, for Bergon drops in references to Basques, Armenians, Sikhs, Italians, American Indians, "blacks," and multiple generations of "Mexicans," from longtime Valley residents to "braceros." In terms of the class dynamics in the novel, it is the Okies, and Sonny in particular, that Bergon interrogates in *Jesse's Ghost*. As Gerald Haslam points out in his essay "What About the Okies?,"

> the influx of Okie kids in valley schools in the late 30s and into the 40s posed a threat to the often unacknowledged, but inflexible class structure of rural areas because they were whites in roles traditionally relegated to nonwhites. One result was that Okies became the victims of stereotyping as rigid as other minority groups faced, perhaps even more so.[8]

From the opening page we see ethnic tension and alliances at work. Sonny's first-person narration marks him as an "Okie" from the outset. He begins with an attempt at formality, which quickly slips into the southern feel of Okie conversation: " 'I will haunt you when I'm dead,' my mother told me all the time when I was a kid, yet the person who haunts me now is

---

7   "Streets of Bakersfield," Buck Owens and Dwight Yoakam, on Dwight Yoakam, *Buenas Noches from a Lonely Room*, Reprise Records, 1988.
8   Gerald Haslam, *The Other California: The Great Central Valley in Life and Letters* (Reno: University of Nevada Press, 1994), 115.

the friend I loved more than my momma or my daddy or even my own brother. His name was Jesse Floyd."[9] With the arrival of the mother's voice, still in the opening paragraph, we enter the language of the Joads, as Sonny's language slips from "mother" to "momma" and then "daddy."

When a "tough pachuco," the older Ray Castaneda, threatens to beat young Sonny, Jesse appears after school to fight for him. As this scene suggests, Okie kids' low status makes them vulnerable to tough "Mexican" kids seeking status of their own. And in the Central Valley status and manhood were earned and expressed physically and through fighting. As Sonny recalls this episode, his memory takes him to their bodily differences. Ray has "eyes like dull aggies," while Jesse's eyes are "baby blue," and although Jesse was "kind of scrawny," he was "scrappy and fast."[10] Sonny's description of Ray's eyes recalls schoolyard games of marbles with Ray's eyes, brown, hard, and impenetrable, like the agate or "aggie" marble. Sonny's figurative language comes from the local and social world of the playground. Here, the antagonism is racialized, but valley residents of Mexican descent and Okies share history and status as much as they differ. Okie boys and men must defend their culture and they wear their heritage as a badge of honor. They might not have any money and they might perform the lowest of manual labor, but they have pride and they are fierce. And they are physical. Through the course of the narrative, although we see fortunes rise and fall and rise, Sonny and Jesse hang on to their physicality as an essential part of who they are. They might get better jobs, they might trade up for higher status women, but their way of apprehending their place and the people in it is bodily.

Throughout the novel, Sonny obsessively focuses on status: the hierarchies of social class, race, and ethnicity in his homeland around Madera, in the San Joaquin Valley. And, as is often the case, those most victimized by stereotyping are often those who cling to those hierarchies most tenaciously. Sonny frequently reads the problem of "class" through the lens of race, ethnicity, and gender. While other characters might express hierarchies verbally, Sonny registers racial, ethnic, class and gender difference as embodied. In *Ordinary Affects*, anthropologist Kathleen Stewart reminds us "the body is both the persistent site of self-recognition and the thing that always betrays us. It dreams of redemption, but it knows better than that too."[11]

---

9   Frank Bergon, *Jesse's Ghost* (Berkeley, CA: Heyday, 2011), 1.
10   Ibid., 1-2.
11   Kathleen Stewart, *Ordinary Affects* (Durham, NC: Duke University Press, 2007), 114.

Sonny apprehends his world sensually. He recounts the stuff of his everyday life, focusing on one summer that comes to determine the course of his life and the death of his best friend Jesse. Following Kathleen Stewart, I want to attend here to affective moments in the text, and recalling Ben Highmore's work on aesthetics and everyday life, I want to hold in solution, as it were, one of his central claims: "our feelings, emotions and passions that seem so 'private' and 'internal' are, in actuality, social-material forces that circulate externally. . . . It is the world that has got under our skin and has stirred us to the core."*12*

When the novel opens, Sonny remains obsessed with a past that led him to kill his best friend. Years later, after doing time, and remarriage, Sonny has moved up the economic scale, to the foothills, literally above his valley past, to a home "a lot nicer than the houses of those ranchers our dads used to work for."*13* But in spite of limited physical mobility due to diabetes, old injuries, and weight gain, Sonny still regards his world through his body, and through sex. Early in the novel, Sonny's second wife Lynette announces that she is leaving him. When Sonia, his first wife, left him and took up again with Jesse, Sonny's response was physical and lethal violence. Here, he understands the present marital crisis to be another instance where he is "second pickings":

> Now the same damn thing was happening with Lynette. She'd met a doctor, probably, someone with education and class, or maybe just another nurse now that half of them are men, or an anesthesiologist or an orderly or a psychologist—the goddamn hospital was full of men for her picking. Full of beds, too. No telling who she ended up with. Last time I was there hardly no one spoke English.*14*

Class anxiety, " a doctor, probably," moves to sexual anxiety, the "goddamn hospital" is full of men, and beds, to racism: no one speaks English. While logic quickly flies out the window here, what we see is a movement from the social—Lynette will "trade up" economically and socially—to the sensual—Lynette's environment is populated with men, all kinds of men,

---

12   Ben Highmore, *Ordinary Lives: Studies in the Everyday* (New York: Routledge, 2011), 33.
13   *Jesse's Ghost*, 3.
14   Ibid., 40.

even low-status, non-English-speaking men, and all of them are thinking only of sex and beds and not their jobs or illnesses. In other words, they all react only sexually to Lynette, just as Sonny seems to.

The imbrications of class, race, and sexuality return in Sonny's recollection of the summer, after his senior year in high school that is crucial to his fate. He works on the Etcheverry Ranch, a veritable United Nations, with an Okie contingent that includes Jesse, Sonny's stepfather Dewey, Sonny's mother and brother, who live on the ranch; various workers of Mexican descent, some who have been there a lifetime, some migrant; the ghost of a Sikh irrigator; a few cowboys; some black workers; and the Etcheverrys--the second and third generations of Basques on the land. Distinctions here are complex: the owner and his son perform physical labor alongside their wage laborers, but Sam owns the ranch that Mitch is presumed to inherit, as Sam did. Their private lives are on display to the workers as they all share physical space, blurring distinctions between workplace and home, public and private.

On a hot and windy day, Sid and Rackenback, two black workers, resist a job that the boss, Sam, doles out. Sonny watches the exchange as much as he listens to it, and notices how the elder of the two workers expresses his resistance. First, when Sam tells them he has a different job for them that day, and one that is bound to be more miserable than the one planned, Rackenback replies, "We got to finish up them weeds in the big cotton piece before the water gets on them."[15] While true, it is not what the boss wants, and when Sam insists that they switch jobs, Rackenback "snatched up the dirt from the ground and flung it into the air, watching it blow sideways, to show Sam it was too windy to be grinding hay." The gesture takes up where the verbal leaves off, and for workers, the gesture suggests rather than argues. The two men do the job they are told to, and "[a]fter they got paid, they started arguing about who worked harder and stopped the car to fight about it."[16] Seeing the men fighting just off the ranch, Sam takes Sonny to stop them, but not before each man has been cut by the makeshift weapons. Sid has been sent home, but they take Rackenback, the older man, to the ranch house where Sam's wife, a nurse, can fix him up.

---

15   Ibid., 96.
16   Ibid.

We drove Rackenback to the ranch house where Ana's
momma pressed a dishtowel against his bleeding forehead
and walked him to the back bathroom. Sam told me to
go with them to make sure there wasn't any trouble.

"You tell Sid to let me look at his arm tomor-
row," she said. "I don't want him getting an infection."

"Yes ma'am," Rackenback said in a voice that
sounded strange. I'd known Rackenback for a couple
of years but hadn't ever heard him talking to a woman
before. It was like he was saying someone else's words in
someone else's voice. He grinned the whole time Ana's
momma put in the stitches. . . .

"When us colored folks gets to fighting, Mrs.
Etcheverry, there's no stopping us. If someone yells,
'Fried chicken,' and someone else yells, 'Fight,' we're
going to the fight." I'd never heard him say things like
that neither.[17]

As Sonny had learned years earlier, the Etcheverrys don't create hard
boundaries between private space and workspace on the ranch, and
workers may enter their home. But some sense of discomfort, racialized
here, prompts Sam to send Sonny along to the bathroom with Mrs.
Etcheverry and Rackenback. Everybody seems to recognize this, but
again the cues are largely affective ones. In a bathroom with the boss's
wife and a coworker, also white, sent to keep an eye on him, Rackenback
shuffles into the role of a black man in the Jim Crow South. In the private,
intimate, and domestic space of the owner's bathroom with the owner's
wife, Rackenback abases himself, when that morning he had resisted the
boss's orders, and moments earlier he had violently defended his honor.
Rackenback reminds Sonny of another black man, one who protected
him, brought him into his home, for food, but, uncomfortable, he never
entered the Okies' or "any white person's home. That was a true black
person back then."[18] The scene mirrors Sonny's own anxieties about the
roles of class and ethnicity in his relationships with the Etcheverrys. As a
worker whose family lives on the ranch, Sonny sees and hears the intimate
lives of the ranch owners. He sees Mrs. Etcheverry, drunk and lurid in her
nightgown; he works and plays alongside Mitch, the owner's son, and he

---

17   Ibid., 98.
18   Ibid., 99.

has sex with the underage daughter, Ana. Sonny, already uncomfortable about the class difference between them, transfers the rigid social hierarchies into racial ones. Against Rackenback, he aligns himself as white rather than as fellow laborer. In love with Ana, Sonny asks Sam for her hand in marriage. Sam tells Sonny that Ana is too spoiled for him and they should not speak of it again. Sam's reply recalls the power dynamics at work with Sid and Rackenback: when employees and employers have competing desires, each chooses to avoid direct confrontation, but each is aware of the hierarchies present in their relationships.

Sonny comprehends the situation in terms of class and identity: he is a laborer and an Okie. Sonny, like Rackenback, has been inside the big house, Sonny has been a sexual threat to the family's position, and has, in terms of public behavior, known his place. He never mentions his affair with Ana to her brother Mitch, he never mentions marriage again, and he imagines that Ana takes up with (and eventually marries) his best friend and rival Jesse because of Jesse's superior physical prowess and social skills. Sonny might not have the vocabulary to analyze this complex negotiation of power, but he feels it, difference as a shadow that comes over both him and Rackenback.

Not only does the scene with Rackenback mirror Sonny's status on the ranch, but also it mirrors Jesse's. Jesse, an Okie, charms women of higher status with his sweet talk and big smile. Rackenback's "Uncle Tom" performance differs from Jesse's in degree, but not in kind. Sonny fights against his own low status with his fists and through sexual relations with women of higher status, but as a man of feeling rather than words, he cannot recognize, in Highmore's words, "that [his] feelings, emotions and passions that seem so 'private' and 'internal' are, in actuality, social-material forces that circulate externally." For Sonny, physical expression of masculinity seemed a way to cross class boundaries, but it is only when his physical prowess declines that he can begin to unstick himself from the obsession with status that keeps him alienated and unable to inhabit the present.

While Sonny's identification with Jesse as best friend, rival, ideal, and object of love reinforces his sense of his own low status, always either second choice or loser, his relationship with Mitch offers him a sense of perspective, helps him find and choose additional identities, and breaks his isolation. Mitch, third generation in the Valley and presumptive heir to the Etcheverry Ranch, occupies a class position above Sonny and so has privileges Sonny lacks, but it is his difference from Sonny that offers a perspectival shift necessary for Sonny's survival and muted redemption. Both Jesse and Sonny make a series of assumptions about Mitch's status and his prospects. While Mitch labors alongside his Okie peers, he has his own modest, but private housing, a cabin filled with books and classical records. Mitch has gone to parochial school and then to boarding school, where, however young men settle differences, they do not use their fists. Indeed, the only fight we see Mitch actually involved in is the one he attempts to break up between Jesse and Sonny. Mitch's life doesn't follow the script. To second-generation Okies, Mitch seems set for a life as a landowner and the boss of laborers like Sonny and Jesse, but third generation is no guarantee of a landed legacy. Mitch's father sells the ranch to pay debts, and Mitch must make his own way in the world.

During the course of the novel, Mitch will surprise Sonny in several ways. From high school forward, Mitch has geographical and social mobility. First boarding school, then college took him away from the agriculture-based society of the Valley. When they meet again years after high school and Jesse's murder, Mitch has moderated his behavior and no longer drinks to excess or "cats" around. Living away from the Valley and ranch, away from a place where masculinity is exclusively physically expressed, Mitch has embraced words. Stories. In a series of meetings after Sonny gets out of prison, Mitch surprises, then startles Sonny with both how he has changed, and with stories. Sonny initially frames Mitch's friendship with his wife, Lynette, in terms of sex, but as he changes, Sonny can begin to imagine that they might just be friends from grade school, as Mitch claims.

Years earlier, when Sonny first got out of prison, they encountered each other at a Valley restaurant. Sonny is sure that Mitch will punish him physically for his crime, for having made Mitch's sister a widow. Typically, Sonny summons Mitch outside, then invites Mitch to hit him, to take revenge physically. Sonny has killed Mitch's brother-in-law and physical retribution is fair. But Sonny is surprised that Mitch declines and bears him no animosity.

Like so many scenes critical to both character development and plot, this first post-Jesse encounter occurs at a restaurant. Early in the novel when Mitch has come to talk to Sonny, once Sonny's wife and daughter leave the house, the men go out for dinner. This first meal is at the local casino, and it is Sonny's birthday. Mitch insists on buying the meal, but that means Sonny must dine on Mitch's terms. Instead of the buffet that he prefers, they go to the steakhouse. Mitch orders a big steak, rare. In the Valley, foodways provide a lot of information about heritage, about class, and about work. Later, we learn that the Okie cowboys like their steaks thin and very well done. We can imagine that with his Okie heritage and working-class upbringing, Sonny has learned that beef of questionable quality should always be well done. Mitch's order recalls his privilege. Sonny, with diabetes, orders "the smallest filet and a big side order of roasted vegetables."[19]

During the substantial section of the novel that recalls the summer that is pivotal in Sonny's life, we will see an elaboration of ranch and Valley foodways as the Etcheverrys prepare a big barbeque in honor of Mitch's departure for college. We learn then of Mitch's taste for large rare steaks, as we do of the cowboys' own tastes, of the ethnic heritages implied by the food—steaks, frogs' legs, Rocky Mountain oysters, lasagna. The barbeque brings out the community, and the confounding of social status, apparent to Sonny as he watches and feels the ways sexual desire crosses class boundaries. For Sonny, the night is pivotal, sending him careening toward transgressions and his eventual murder of Jesse.

Near the end of the novel, Mitch has drafted his article about Jesse's murder, and he visits Sonny to fact check and assess Sonny's welfare. Sonny presses Mitch to go visit the old Etcheverry place, sold off to pay Sam's debts. To his surprise, Mitch agrees. Sonny might be ready, at long last, to confront his ghosts, talking through the murder with Mitch, and Mitch, too, might be ready to confront his ghosts—anger at his dead father and his own sense of loss. Mitch proposes lunch at Fresno's Basque Hotel. The name immediately conjures up the famous shrimp potato salad and Sonny agrees. As they spend the day together each will confront the past, their habits of remembering and misremembering, and their ghosts. At the Basque Hotel, when the lunch bell rings, they file in from the bar to the long communal, or boarders' table, for the big family-style meal, mostly men and a handful of women. No shrimp potato salad appears. Sonny tries to wheedle some from the waitress, but the restaurant's rules are rigid. The salad can be ordered only at the individual tables with an à la carte menu. It's served at the boarders' table two days a week. The rules. Here, as on the ranch and in town, there have always been rules. Up to this point in the novel, Sonny has never doubted his memory or his interpretation of events, and this time is no different. Stuck in a story where the old days were always better, Sonny asserts, " 'Ain't nothing the same no more,' and Mitch contradicts, 'It's the same.' "[20]

---

19   Ibid., 12.
20   Ibid, 164.

The men continue to the old ranch and find it radically transformed. While Mitch resists " 'being nostalgic, idealizing the good old days as better than now,' " Sonny recalls his intimacy with the ranch, with the work, and with those who worked it with him. Ghosts come cascading toward him, tumbling out in a single page of text. And with those memories, Sonny begins to enrich and complicate the mythology he has made from his own past. Stories come fast and furious now that he has grounded them as memories, altered like the ranch, and now that he has someone to question both his stories *and* his assumptions. None of the main characters in *Jesse's Ghost* has a strong or supportive family to link them from past to present, to locate them intimately in time and place. They must look to each other for such links. Later, over time, Mitch offers Sonny alternative versions of past events, compelling Sonny to accept a different perspective. When Mitch reads Sonny part of an article he is writing about Jesse, Sonny finds:

> myself listening to Mitch read his story like it wasn't about me but someone like me, and other guys like me. . . . I kept listening, almost relieved in some strange way from what I was hearing, having it be about other people, like a play under the lights in a school auditorium . . .[21]

Hearing his own story, but from a different perspective, helps Sonny see the external circulation of emotions and passions, in Highmore's terms. And that allows him to see Lynette's point of view, a crucial step in their reconciliation. The narrative work, performed by Mitch and Sonny (*and* Bergon) doesn't negate difference, rather it shifts difference from hierarchy and competition to community.

While *Jesse's Ghost* confronts the dark legacies of the Valley, rendering the lethal consequences and limitations of a masculinity based on sex, violence, and individualism, Bergon's recent book, *Two-Buck Chuck & the Marlboro Man*, expands that vision considerably. Here he revisits some of the issues woven into *Jesse's Ghost*, but through interviews, histories, and analysis. And here, he shows what Joan Didion has refused to see. Through interviews with friends, acquaintances, and strangers, Bergon reveals a Great Central Valley that has held onto many Old West values while it has adapted to New West economics and environments. In his roles as interviewer and essayist, Bergon highlights the beneficial core beliefs:

21　Ibid., 187.

an Old West code of toughness and hard work that I
saw my grandparents and parents continue to believe in:
a communal allegiance to Western dreams of freedom
and opportunity, an optimistic fortitude coupled with
physical endurance, a respect for work with your hands,
a disinclination to complain or give up, all the time knowing that the demands of the code in confrontation with
the harsh cyclical reality of agricultural disappointment
might leave you crushed. Or possibly renewed.[22]

In the San Joaquin Valley Bergon finds these old values blending with New
West realities, and in the profiles, he shows resilience and adaptability in
nearly all of his subjects. While in *Jesse's Ghost* the best we can hope for is a
conscious retreat from toxic masculinity and a modicum of spiritual peace,
in the twenty-first-century Valley Bergon shows us clear-eyed realists who
face both past and future without blinking. Class divisions remain, to be
sure, and some of the poorest cities in America hunker down under winter's
tule fog, but the Valley is among the most diverse places in America, family
businesses coexist alongside international corporate giants, and innovators
work to produce agricultural products without ruining the land.

While the main characters in *Jesse's Ghost* all suffer from both an
absence of a supportive family and an enduring community, many of the
people profiled in *Two-Buck Chuck & the Marlboro Man* have managed to
maintain strong family and community ties. Most of these people depend
on others, in family businesses, in long-term business relationships, and
for personal identity. Many of them gain perspective, necessary for their
success and their happiness as Valley residents, by going away for a while.
For winemaker Fred Franzia and his high-level manager Sal Arriola, it is by
attending college outside the valley. Darrell Winfield left the Valley when
ranching diminished and moved his family to Wyoming, where with the
help of his income as the Marlboro Man, he set up a small ranch that
employs multiple family generations. And for many of these people, the
perspectives gained from physical hardship and manual labor have made
them better bosses and better managers of the land. In Bergon's interview-
based profiles, Valley residents speak more often of the "self-recognition"
that comes from embodied knowledge, to borrow again from Kathleen

---

22   Frank Bergon, *Two-Buck Chuck & the Marlboro Man.* (Reno: University of Nevada
      Press, 2019), 9- 10.

Stewart, but unlike *Jesse's Ghost*, there is no novelist here to remind us, again in Stewart's terms that the body also "always betrays us." The differences, then, expressed as embodied in *Jesse's Ghost*, reveal themselves in *Two-Buck Chuck & the Marlboro Man* as historical and perspectival. The collection of profiles and essays continues to parse relationships between Old West and New West taken up in the novel, with an emphasis on the legacies of Old West values and their relevance in the twenty-first-century rural West.

Bergon, working in a different genre here, and with representational goals that differ significantly from Didion's, interviews his subjects, spends time with them at work, and sometimes shares meals with them, allowing him an intimacy that reveals the complexities in each of his subjects. He can address racial, ethnic, and gender difference through his subjects' own behavior and their observations. For example, Nancy Turner Gray, "The Black Ranch Girl," insists that the Madera of her childhood was "a very racist place," that it manifested differently for girls than for boys, especially athletes, and that the small-town schools also insured mixing of races and social classes, as she " 'always said the doctors' kids went to school with the wino's kids. You had to be together.' "[23] Her childhood experiences included informal, but also rigid racial segregation, yet there was also "a strong black community in those days, with black churches, black leaders, black businesses," something she doesn't find as much of in a place that is now "seventy-five percent Hispanic, if not more."[24] While town relationships often followed a de facto code of segregation—she and a friend of Japanese ancestry couldn't play at a white girl's house—the ranch neighbors, all white, were different. " 'We were friends with our white neighbors. . . . At that time, the culture was to treat people with respect who worked hard. My father was a hard worker.' "[25]

Indeed, hard work emerges as a common denominator in most of the profiles. In Part I, titled "Working the Dirt," we meet several Valley residents, highly successful by almost any public measure. Fred Franzia, the genius behind the infamous Charles Shaw, the award-winning and bargain priced wine, a.k.a. "Two-Buck Chuck," comes across as a fiend for work. Friends, acquaintances, employees, and rivals all confirm his "tremendous work ethic."[26] Tenacity, preparation, and creative adaptability contribute to the phenomenal success of Franzia's family business. His family-owned Bronco Wine Company is the largest vineyard owner in the

---

23   Ibid. 119, 122.
24   Ibid., 124
25   Ibid., 125.
26   Ibid., 21.

United States, with 40,000 acres of organic grapes, and the company is both economically and environmentally innovative.

Bergon devotes the next chapter to one of Bronco's high-level managers, Sal Arriola, who crossed the Mexican border illegally with his family when he was three. Arriola grew up working in the fields, but academically adept, he used school as a way to leave manual labor behind. Like Bergon and Franzia, Arriola left the Valley to further his education. A gifted athlete, too, Arriola earned a scholarship to play volleyball at Division I University of California, Santa Barbara. Arriola speaks openly about the complex negotiations around race, class, and ethnicity in the Valley, and heatedly discusses how he came to be accused of mistreating fieldworkers as head of farming for Bronco. As Bergon develops this chapter, he provides other examples of locals embedded in a tradition of family farming, all tarred with the brush of big (heartless) corporate agriculture. The truth here, Bergon insists, is both more complex and more individuated.

Other chapters show readers the Lasgoitys, a Basque ranching family, whose daughter Michele, after twelve years with Hewlett Packard, returns to the Valley, rejoins the family business, and, as a woman, wins Madera County's "Cattleman of the Year."[27] Bergon profiles a self-identified "Korean Okie," African American men and women, Native Americans, and rich men with no thought of selling out and spending their wealth. The old work ethic remains a cornerstone, as Sal Arriola says of his success, " 'Not too many guys are going to outwork me.' "[28]

These essays do more than reveal the complexity of difference in the Great Central Valley and the West—they offer no actual rugged individualists. Each chapter works to undercut or refute dominant mythologies about the American West. In the process, both the ubiquitous mythologies promoted by the long-running Marlboro Man campaigns, as well as the mythologies upheld by Californians such as Joan Didion, lose their grip under the weight of history, statistics, and stories. In *Jesse's Ghost* rugged individualism, along with machismo, proves fatal. In *Two-Buck Chuck & the Marlboro Man* it is largely irrelevant. The Great Central Valley continues to struggle with environmental degradation, income inequality, poverty, urbanization, and the friction of diversity, but Bergon celebrates the hard-working, big-dreaming families and communities that face such challenges together.

---

27   Ibid., 72-74.
28   Ibid., 67.

Many of Bergon's interviews take place over meals. Whether at a small café, a taco stand, a ranch barbeque, a steakhouse, or Fresno's Basque Hotel, Bergon's thematic development often pivots over the course of a meal. Food works as a social leveling device in both the fiction and nonfiction that depicts Valley life. While interviewing Fred Franzia, Bergon takes care to note Franzia's request for a Bloody Mary at a Madera café. At 10:30 a.m., the bar is closed, negotiations ensue, and Franzia manages to get what he needs by ordering both tomato juice and tabasco sauce.

" 'That's what I really want,' he says, 'I like the heat.' "[29] Shared meals allow readers to see Franzia as he engages with employees and friends. Near the close of the essay, Bergon asks about the division of labor in Bronco, the family business. Of working with his cousin, Franzia insists, " 'we do pretty much everything together,' "and offering a "mischievous grin," he adds: " 'But I go where the heat is.' " For Bergon, food binds both members of the community and the narrative.

Which brings me to an essay, "Family Style," that Bergon published in 2001. As we have seen earlier, eating in the company of others creates intimacy, and, as an important part of everyday life, meals offer a place, recalling Ben Highmore, where we can see the "social-material forces circulate externally" while also remaining "private" and "internal." For Bergon, "family style" evokes the "boarders' table" at Basque restaurants in the West, "a long, noisy table with people you might not know and eating food you hadn't ordered."[30] A trip to the Basque Hotel in Fresno evokes memories of many meals from childhood, with the familiar menu and the courses all put out at once for the communal meal. At one meal in adulthood, Bergon, like Sonny, is denied the shrimp potato salad because he is there on the wrong day. Traditions survive, but things change, too. Gone are the photos of Bergon's family, replaced by a "photograph of the owners with ten men who are regulars." Bergon asks how many Basques are in the photo, and the owner replies, " 'Only me.' . . . Four men are Japanese, others are Mexican, and . . . Okie." Another regular pipes up: "They're like family here."[31] And this remark reminds us that "family style" at the boarders' table began as a service for the rooming house upstairs at many of these hotels, a place for "men without families, mostly unmarried Basque sheepherders."[32]

---

29 Ibid., 17.
30 Frank Bergon, "Family Style," *Gastronomica* 1, no. 4 (Fall 2001): 16.
31 Ibid., 20.
32 Ibid., 16.

For Bergon, the "True West," the blending of Old Wests and New, honors a multiethnic, multiracial past, supports families as it allows them to adapt and thrive, and looks for continuities between the old and the new. In his California writing, Bergon portrays those who have been dismissed or remain invisible in work by writers such as Didion, in popular culture, and in contemporary letters. It is through the events of everyday life— adversity, work, eating—that his characters reveal their identities and their ethics. The "True West" of the Great Central Valley is found, not at the buffet or the drive-through, but at the boarders' table, where diners "just eat on, for the living and for the dead, silently aware of bonds stronger than those of ethnicity and geography. So we eat on, family style."[33]

WORKS CITED

Bergon, Frank. "Family Style." *Gastronomica* 1, no. 4 (Fall 2001): 16-20.

_____. *Jesse's Ghost.* Berkeley, CA: Heyday, 2011.

_____. Review of *Small Bird, Tell Me: Stories of Greek Immigrants in Utah.* By *Helen Papanikolas (Athens: Swallow Press/Ohio University Press), 1993. Western American Literature* 30, no. 3 (Fall 1995):295-296.

_____. *Two-Buck Chuck & the Marlboro Man: The New Old West.* Reno: University of Nevada Press, 2019.

Haslam, Gerald. *The Other California: The Great Central Valley in Life and Letters.* Reno: University of Nevada Press, 1994.

Highmore, Ben. *Ordinary Lives: Studies in the Everyday.* New York: Routledge, 2011.

Joy, Homer. "Streets of Bakersfield," 1972. Dwight Yoakam, *Buenas Noches from a Lonely Room.* Reprise Records, 1988.

Stewart, Kathleen. *Ordinary Affects.* Durham, NC: Duke University Press, 2007.

---

33 Ibid., 20.

CONTRIBUTORS

IÑAKI ARRIETA BARO has served since 2015 as the head of the Jon Bilbao Basque Library at the University of Nevada, Reno, a specialized unit supporting researchers from all around the world interested in Basque Studies. He focuses on preserving and providing access to the documentary heritage of the Basque Diaspora in the United States, mainly through digital and outreach projects, working with the Basque community to acquire new archival collections to help better understand the Basque experience in Nevada and the West. Since 2017, Arrieta Baro has worked closely with Frank Bergon in transferring his literary and pictorial collection to the Basque Library.

FRANK BERGON was born in Ely, Nevada, and grew up on a ranch in California's San Joaquin Valley. He has published twelve books—four novels, a critical study, two books of essays, and five edited collections. His Nevada trilogy consists of *Shoshone Mike, The Temptations of St. Ed & Brother S*, and *Wild Game*, three novels spanning a century from the Shoshone massacre of 1911 to the current battle over nuclear waste in the Nevada desert. His California trilogy consists of *Jesse's Ghost, Two-Buck Chuck & The Marlboro Man*, and *The Toughest Kid We Knew*, all focusing on the San Joaquin Valley, including Basques and Béarnais of his own heritage. He is also the author of *Stephen Crane's Artistry*, the editor of the Penguin Classics edition of *The Journals of Lewis and Clark, The Western Writings of Stephen Crane, The Wilderness Reader, A Sharp Lookout: Selected Nature Essays of John Burroughs*, and the coeditor with Zeese Papanikolas of *Looking Far West: The Search for the American West in History, Myth, and Literature*. He has taught at the University of Washington and for many years at Vassar College. He is a member of the Nevada Writers Hall of Fame.

NANCY S. COOK is Professor of English at the University of Montana, Missoula, where she teaches courses in Western American studies and ecocriticism. Her publications include work on California writers, water policy and the West, and ranching. She is a Past President of the Western

Literature Association. Currently she is at work on a book-length study of twentieth-century U.S. ranching cultures.

SYLVAN GOLDBERG is an assistant professor in the English Department at Colorado College, where he teaches classes on American literature and the environmental humanities. He has published essays on affective ecocriticism, William Faulkner's environmental imagination, and the centrality of environment in Western American literature, among other topics. He is completing a manuscript on overlaps between sentimentalism and the life sciences in nineteenth-century U.S. culture.

WILLIAM HEATH has taught American literature and creative writing at Kenyon, Transylvania, Vassar, the University of Seville, and Mt. St. Mary's University. He has published two chapbooks, *Night Moves in Ohio* and *Leaving Seville*, and a book of poetry, *The Walking Man*; three novels: *The Children Bob Moses Led*, *Blacksnake's Path*, and *Devil Dancer*; an award-winning work of history, *William Wells and the Struggle for the Old Northwest*, and a collection of interviews, *Conversations with Robert Stone*. In addition, he has published some twenty literary and historical essays in academic journals and literary reviews.

XABIER IRUJO is the director of the Center for Basque Studies at the University of Nevada, Reno, where he is professor of genocide studies. He was the first guest research scholar of the Manuel Irujo Chair at the University of Liverpool and has taught seminars on genocide and cultural genocide at Boise State University and at the University of California, Santa Barbara. He holds three masters degrees in linguistics, history, and philosophy and has two Ph.D.s in history and philosophy. Dr. Irujo has widely lectured at various American and European universities and published on issues related to Basque history and politics. He has specialized during his career in genocide studies, researching periods of Basque history related to both physical and cultural extermination. He has mentored several graduate students and he is a member of the editorial board of four academic presses. Dr. Irujo has authored more than fifteen books and a number of articles in specialized journals and has received awards and distinctions at national and international levels. His recent books include

Gernika: Genealogy of a Lie (Sussex Academic Press, 2019) and *Gernika 1937: The Market Day Massacre* (University of Nevada Press, 2015).

MONIKA MADINABEITIA is an associate professor in the Humanities and Education division (HUHEZI) at Mondragon University. Her main teaching area is related to culture, with an emphasis on cross-culturalism and e/migration. She focused her dissertation on Frank Bergon´s fiction within the framework of Literature of the American West. She teaches in the Education degree as well as in the degree of Audiovisual Communication. She is part of the international research team Rewest and has participated in organizing several international conferences and seminars at the University of the Basque Country. She is in charge of the Annual Literary Encounters of Basque Literature since 2010 and has been on the committee for the Basque Awards for essays in Basque organized by the Basque Government since 2017.

DAVID MEANS was born and raised in Michigan. His second collection of stories, *Assorted Fire Events*, earned the Los Angeles Times Book Prize for fiction, and his third, *The Secret Goldfish*, was short-listed for the Frank O'Connor International Short Story Prize. His fourth, *The Spot*, was selected as a 2010 Notable Book by *The New York Times* and won an O. Henry Prize. He was a recipient of a 2013 Guggenheim Fellowship. His first novel, *Hystopia*, was published in 2016 to wide acclaim, and was long-listed for the Man Booker Prize. Means's fiction has appeared in *The Best American Short Stories*, *The Best American Mystery Stories*, *The O. Henry Prize Stories*, and numerous other publications. His latest collection of stories, *Instructions for a Funeral*, was published in 2019 by Farrar, Straus and Giroux. He lives in Nyack, New York, and is a professor of English at Vassar College.

ZEESE PAPANIKOLAS was born in Salt Lake City, Utah, in 1942. He was a Stegner Fellow in Creative Writing at Stanford in 1965-66, where he met Frank Bergon. He collaborated with Bergon on the anthology *Looking Far West: The Search for the American West in History, Myth, and Literature*. He is the author of *Buried Unsung*, a biography of the Greek immigrant organizer Louis Tikas, who was killed at the Ludlow Massacre in 1914, and three books on American Culture: *Trickster in the Land of Dreams*, *American Silence*, and *An American Cakewalk*.

DAVID RIO is a professor of American literature at the University of the Basque Country, where he has been teaching for the last thirty years. His research interests are within the field of American Studies, with an emphasis on diaspora studies, regional literatures, and especially Western American writing and Basque American literature. He is the author of *El proceso de la violencia en la narrativa de Robert Penn Warren* (1995), *Robert Laxalt: The Voice of the Basques in American Literature* (2007), and *New Literary Portraits of the American West: Contemporary Nevada Fiction* (2014). David Rio has also published articles on contemporary Western American literature, southern literature, and Basque American authors in journals such as *Atlantis: Journal of the Spanish Association for Anglo-American Studies*, and *Western American Literature*, among others. He has been a guest lecturer at the University of Nevada, Reno, the University of California, Santa Barbara, and Vassar College, as well as at several European universities. He has served as member of the AEDEAN (Asociación Española de Estudios Anglo-Norteamericanos) Board and the EAAS (European Association for American Studies) Board from 2008 to 2012.

JOSEBA ZULAIKA is Professor Emeritus at the Center for Basque Studies, University of Nevada, Reno. He graduated in philosophy at the University of Deusto and received a Ph.D. in Cultural Anthropology from Princeton University. During the course of his studies, Dr. Zulaika has conducted fieldwork and published ethnographies of deep-sea fishermen, farmers, soldiers, terrorists, hunters, and artists. He has published on terrorism and counterterrorism, including *Basque Violence: Metaphor and Sacrament*; *Terror and Taboo: The Follies, Fables and Faces of Terrorism* (with William Douglass); *Terrorism: The Self-Fulfilling Prophecy*; *That Old Bilbao Moon: The Passion and Resurrection of a City*; and most recently *Hellfire from Paradise Ranch: On the Frontlines of Drone Warfare*.